When the Time
Was Fulfilled

When the Time Was Fulfilled

Christmas Meditations

Eberhard Arnold
Christoph Blumhardt
Alfred Delp

Plough Publishing House

Published by Plough Publishing House
Walden, New York
Robertsbridge, England
Elsmore, Australia
www.plough.com

First Edition, 1964
Second Edition, 2007
20 19 18 17 16 15 14   3 4 5 6 7 8 9 10 11

This book is a revised and expanded collection based on the first edition:
a collection originally put together by Emmy Arnold. The Scripture
passages are based on the New International Version of the Bible.

A catalog record for this book is available from the British Library.

Library of Congress Cataloging-in-Publication Data

Arnold, Eberhard, 1883-1935.
  [Selections. English. 2007]
  When the time was fulfilled : Christmas meditations / Eberhard
Arnold, Christoph Blumhardt, Alfred Delp.-- 2nd ed.
        p. cm.
  ISBN-13: 978–0–87486–940–8
  1. Advent--Meditations. 2. Christmas--Meditations. I. Blumhardt,
Christoph, 1842-1919. II. Delp, Alfred. III. Title.
  BV40.A7 2007
  242'.33--dc22

                          2007035109

Printed in the USA

He who would be born of God
must be mindful of how Christ's
birth took place.

Eberhard Arnold

Contents

Advent

Expectation

Glad Tidings

God with Us

Introduction

How would Christ want us to prepare for Christmas? In what way might he want us to remember his birth? This is the central concern of this book.

Obviously, Christians around the world, as they have throughout the ages, celebrate Christmas differently. Traditions, customs, rituals, and symbols are as varied as the people who engage them. As meaningful as these expressions are, the supposition within this book is that outward forms and practices, whether they are holiday preparations or religious observances, bear little importance if Christ himself is not born again in our midst. Celebration is a distraction if not accompanied by conversion; remembering is futile if we fail to experience redemption.

Christmas is indeed something to anticipate. It is a season of joy for good reason: it is the news of a Savior being born, of light breaking into darkness, of God's peace and goodwill to all. But joy is more than merriment. For those who only want to have a good time or a feeling of togetherness, Christmas brings little more than a temporary feeling of cheer. Afterwards, life goes on as before. But for the one who feels bankrupt, without real meaning or hope – either for themselves or for the world – for the one who senses that something is terribly wrong with the way things are, Christmas can be genuinely life changing.

Sadhu Sundar Singh, a mystic in India at the turn of the last century, was once sitting along the bank of a river. He drew out of the water a beautiful, round stone and smashed it. The inside was bone dry. The water had not penetrated it, for the rock had hardened itself. "It is just like that with all the 'Christian' people of the West," he observed. "They have for centuries been surrounded by Christianity, but the Master has not penetrated them."

Far too many of us come near to the manger, but refuse to let the Christ child penetrate our lives. This is why things remain as they are. The question before us is this: Will the Child come into the dusty, dirty cavern of our lives? Or will we just unthinkingly immerse ourselves in Christmas sights and sounds, content that all is shine?

The meditations in this collection are meant solely to prepare us to meet Christ anew. They point us to the fact that the God of the universe finds himself most at home in people who feel their need and are personally ready to come to the manger. Christmas is glad tidings indeed, but only for those who are starkly honest with themselves and recognize that life must change.

These selections are written by three men who struggled hard and long to find, in the words of Søren Kierkegaard, "the contemporary Christ." They testify by their lives that the birth of Jesus is more than history – it is a reality.

Christoph Blumhardt, a German pastor and religious socialist in the late nineteenth and early twentieth centuries, experienced the victorious power of Christ over sickness and demons that can possess and oppress individuals and entire congregations. The reality of Christ came dramatically and sweepingly into the village of Möttlingen, where his father was pastor, and continued on in his own ministry of healing in Bad Boll. Although rejected by his peers, there were hundreds, if not thousands, of needy souls reborn and transformed through his ministry. The Christ child was "born again and again."

Eberhard Arnold, a German theologian, publisher, and speaker, left the religious establishment and social status quo in Germany altogether and in Franciscan-style poverty formed in 1920 a community of brothers and sisters. They lived together entirely on the teachings in the Sermon on the Mount. For Arnold, every disciple must become "mindful of how Christ's birth took place." This "how" of Christ's birth reveals the true source of Christmas joy, and it alone points the way to God's kingdom and makes it real.

Alfred Delp was a pastor in Munich who secretly helped Jews who were escaping Hitler's Germany to Switzerland. Condemned as a traitor for his opposition to Hitler, Delp wrote the pieces in this collection in a Nazi prison shortly before he was hanged in 1945. The Gestapo offered Delp his freedom if he would leave the Jesuits, but he refused. Like Christ, he humbled himself and was obedient unto death.

In their own, unique fashion, each author helps us to understand what it means to prepare for Christ's birth today. Yes, long ago in a small town called Bethlehem, God acted decisively in history. But, as the apostle Paul writes, "Now is the time of God's favor, now is the day of salvation" (2 Cor. 6:2). The joyful news of Christmas is that we too, like those at the first Christmas, can experience the glory of God. The Word can become flesh and live among us. We too, as the apostle John writes, can receive "one blessing after another" (Jn. 1:16). Into the darkness of our lives and our world the light can still shine.

Charles E. Moore

The Christmas Story

According to the Gospels

Before the beginning of time there was the Word, and the Word was with God, and the Word was God. He was with God in the beginning.

Through him all things were made; without him nothing was made that has been made. In him was life, and that life was the light of all people. The light shines in the darkness, but the darkness has neither understood nor overcome it.

There came a man who was sent from God; his name was John. He came as a witness to testify concerning that light, so that through him all people might believe. He himself was not the light; he came only as a witness to the light. The true light that gives light to every person, Christ Jesus himself, was coming into the world.

Jesus came into the world, and though the world was made through him, the world did not recognize him. He came to that which was his own, but his own did not receive him. Yet to all who received him, to those who believed in his name, he gave the right to become children of God – children born not of natural descent, nor of human decision or a husband's will, but born of God.

The Word became flesh and made his dwelling among us. We have seen Christ's glory, the glory of the One and Only, who came from the Father, full of grace and truth.

Before Christ took on human flesh, and after an angel had visited Zechariah, a priest in Jerusalem, God sent the angel Gabriel to Nazareth, a town in Galilee, to a virgin pledged to be married to a man named Joseph, a descendant of David. The virgin's name was Mary. The angel went to her and said, "Greetings, you who are highly favored! The Lord is with you."

Mary was greatly troubled at his words and wondered what kind of greeting this might be. But the angel said to her, "Do not be afraid, Mary, you have found favor with God. You will be with child and give birth to a son, and you are to give him the name Jesus. He will be great and will be called the Son of the Most High. The Lord God will give him the throne of his father David, and he will reign over the house of Jacob forever; his kingdom will never end."

"How will this be," Mary asked the angel, "since I am a virgin?"

The angel answered, "The Holy Spirit will come upon you, and the power of the Most High will overshadow you. So the holy one to be born will be called the Son of God. Even Elizabeth your relative is going to have a child in her old age, and she who was said to be barren is in her sixth month. For nothing is impossible with God."

"I am the Lord's servant," Mary answered. "May it be to me as you have said." Then the angel left her.

At that time Mary got ready and hurried to a town in the hill country of Judea, where she entered Zechariah's home and greeted his wife, Elizabeth. When Elizabeth heard Mary's greeting, the baby whom she was carrying in her womb leaped, and Elizabeth was filled with the Holy Spirit. In a loud voice she exclaimed: "Blessed are you among women, and blessed is the child you will bear! But why am I so favored, that the mother of my Lord should come to me? As soon as the sound of your greeting reached my ears, the baby in my womb leaped for joy. Blessed is she who has believed that what the Lord has said to her will be accomplished!"

And Mary said:

My soul glorifies the Lord
and my spirit rejoices in God my Savior,
for he has been mindful
of the humble state of his servant.
From now on all generations will call me blessed,
for the Mighty One has done great things for
   me—
holy is his name.
His mercy extends to those who fear him,
from generation to generation.
He has performed mighty deeds with his arm;
he has scattered those who are proud in their
   inmost thoughts.
He has brought down rulers from their thrones
but has lifted up the humble.
He has filled the hungry with good things
but has sent the rich away empty.
He has helped his servant Israel,
remembering to be merciful
to Abraham and his descendants forever,
even as he said to our fathers.

Mary stayed with Elizabeth for about three months
and then returned home.

Now this is how the birth of Jesus Christ actually
came about: His mother Mary was pledged to be

married to Joseph, but before they came together, she was found to be with child through the Holy Spirit. Because Joseph her husband was a righteous man and did not want to expose her to public disgrace, he had in mind to divorce her quietly.

But after he had considered this, an angel of the Lord appeared to him in a dream and said, "Joseph son of David, do not be afraid to take Mary home as your wife, because what is conceived in her is from the Holy Spirit. She will give birth to a son, and you are to give him the name Jesus, because he will save his people from their sins."

All this took place to fulfill what the Lord had said through the prophet: "The virgin will be with child and will give birth to a son, and they will call him Immanuel" – which means, "God with us."

When Joseph woke up, he did what the angel of the Lord had commanded him and took Mary home as his wife. But he had no union with her until she gave birth to a son. And he gave him the name Jesus.

In those days Caesar Augustus issued a decree that a census should be taken of the entire Roman world. (This was the first census that took place while Quirinius was governor of Syria.) And everyone went to his own town to register.

So Joseph also went up from the town of Nazareth in Galilee to Judea, to Bethlehem the town of David, because he belonged to the house and line of David. He went there to register with Mary, who was pledged to be married to him and was expecting a child. While they were there, the time came for the baby to be born, and she gave birth to her firstborn, a son. She wrapped him in cloths and placed him in a manger, because there was no room for them in the inn.

And there were shepherds living out in the fields nearby, keeping watch over their flocks at night. An angel of the Lord appeared to them, and the glory of the Lord shone around them, and they were terrified. But the angel said to them, "Do not be afraid. I bring you good news of great joy that will be for all the people. Today in the town of David a Savior has been born to you; he is Christ the Lord. This will be a sign to you: You will find a baby wrapped in cloths and lying in a manger."

Suddenly a great company of the heavenly host appeared with the angel, praising God and saying,

Glory to God in the highest,
and on earth peace to men on whom his favor rests.

When the angels had left them and gone into heaven, the shepherds said to one another, "Let's go to Bethlehem and see this thing that has happened, which the Lord has told us about."

So they hurried off and found Mary and Joseph, and the baby, who was lying in the manger. When they had seen him, they spread the word concerning what had been told them about this child, and all who heard it were amazed at what the shepherds said to them. But Mary treasured up all these things and pondered them in her heart. The shepherds returned, glorifying and praising God for all the things they had heard and seen, which were just as they had been told.

On the eighth day, when it was time to circumcise him, he was named Jesus, the name the angel had given him before he had been conceived.

When the time of their purification according to the Law of Moses had been completed, Joseph and Mary took him to Jerusalem to present him to the Lord (as it is written in the Law of the Lord, "Every firstborn male is to be consecrated to the Lord"), and to offer a sacrifice in keeping with what is said in the Law of the Lord: "a pair of doves or two young pigeons."

Now there was a man in Jerusalem called Simeon, who was righteous and devout. He was waiting for the consolation of Israel, and the Holy Spirit was upon him. It had been revealed to him by the Holy Spirit that he would not die before he had seen the Lord's Christ. Moved by the Spirit, he went into the temple courts. When the parents brought in the child Jesus to do for him what the custom of the Law required, Simeon took him in his arms and praised God, saying:

> Sovereign Lord, as you have promised,
> now dismiss your servant in peace.
> For my eyes have seen your salvation,
> which you have prepared in the sight of all
>   people,
> a light for revelation to the Gentiles
> and for glory to your people Israel.

The child's father and mother marveled at what was said about him. Then Simeon blessed them and said to Mary, his mother: "This child is destined to cause the falling and rising of many in Israel, and to be a sign that will be spoken against, so that the thoughts of many hearts will be revealed. And a sword will pierce your own soul too."

There was also a prophetess, Anna, the daughter of Phanuel, of the tribe of Asher. She was very old; she had lived with her husband seven years after her marriage, and then was a widow until she was eighty-four. She never left the temple but worshiped night and day, fasting and praying. Coming up to them at that very moment, she gave thanks to God and spoke about the child to all who were looking forward to the redemption of Jerusalem.

After Jesus was born in Bethlehem in Judea, during the time of King Herod, Magi, or wise men, from the East came to Jerusalem and asked, "Where is the one who has been born king of the Jews? We saw his star in the east and have come to worship him."

When King Herod heard this he was disturbed, and all Jerusalem with him. When he had called together all the people's chief priests and teachers of the law, he asked them where the Christ was to be born. "In Bethlehem in Judea," they replied, "for this is what the prophet has written:

> But you, Bethlehem, in the land of Judah,
> are by no means least among the rulers of Judah;
> for out of you will come a ruler
> who will be the shepherd of my people Israel."

Then Herod called the Magi secretly and found out from them the exact time the star had appeared. He sent them to Bethlehem and said, "Go and make a careful search for the child. As soon as you find him, report to me, so that I too may go and worship him."

After they had heard the king, they went on their way, and the star they had seen in the east went ahead of them until it stopped over the place where the child was. When they saw the star, they were overjoyed. On coming to the house, they saw the child with his mother Mary, and they bowed down and worshiped him. Then they opened their treasures and presented him with gifts of gold and of incense and of myrrh. And having been warned in a dream not to go back to Herod, they returned to their country by another route.

When they had gone, an angel of the Lord appeared to Joseph in a dream. "Get up," he said, "take the child and his mother and escape to Egypt. Stay there until I tell you, for Herod is going to search for the child to kill him."

So he got up, took the child and his mother during the night and left for Egypt, where he stayed until the death of Herod. And so was fulfilled what the Lord had said through the prophet: "Out of Egypt I called my son."

When Herod realized that he had been outwitted by the Magi, he was furious, and he gave orders to kill all the boys in Bethlehem and its vicinity who were two years old and under, in accordance with the time he had learned from the Magi. Then what was said through the prophet Jeremiah was fulfilled:

A voice is heard in Ramah,
weeping and great mourning,
Rachel weeping for her children
and refusing to be comforted,
because they are no more.

After Herod died, an angel of the Lord appeared in a dream to Joseph in Egypt and said, "Get up, take the child and his mother and go to the land of Israel, for those who were trying to take the child's life are dead."

So he got up, took the child and his mother and went to the land of Israel. But when he heard that Archelaus was reigning in Judea in place of his father Herod, he was afraid to go there. Having been warned in a dream, and having done everything required by the law, Joseph returned with his wife Mary to Galilee to their own town of Nazareth. So was fulfilled what was said through the prophets: "He will be called a Nazarene." And the child grew and became strong; he was filled with wisdom, and the grace of God was upon him.

This is a Gospel harmony based on the New International Version of the Bible.

Advent

1

The Eve of Advent

In the past God spoke... through the prophets at many times and in various ways.

Hebrews 1:1

Advent is a time in which we share in the longing of all those who lived in the distant past. We must feel how, in their suffering and struggle, they too longed for redemption and liberation, for unity, for peace, for a golden age. They waited for a manifestation of God's love and unity, for a breaking in of his justice among the nations. We must learn to put ourselves in the place of all those in Israel who were waiting for him who was to come. This One was to free them from their need and disruption, from sin, from their lack of fellowship, from their lost condition, so that they might come to God.

This faithful, eager longing expects still more from the One who is to come. We are convinced that there is One who will create peace and social justice for everyone. We expect him and thus long with a humble spirit that his rulership is recognized in every country. And when this happens, he will turn bloody weapons into tools for work, and we shall become true brothers and sisters. The Messiah-King of peace and justice, the world ruler of love and joy will reign! This was the expectation of old, and this is what we think of when we approach the season of Jesus' birth.

Like the prophets of old, we too need to feel the outrageous injustice that exists within society today and how heavy a burden this is. Injustice ought to stir our hearts; the lack of peace in a world bristling with weapons should haunt us. Disunity exists not only among nations, but also in the midst of every nation. There are far too many unjust governments today. A grave evil results when all our honest labor is supplanted by factories and modern technology. The workers are like living corpses who have no influence on the shaping of the economy, even though it is from their hands that all the things come which are enjoyed and distributed and sold.

Dissensions between classes, races, and ethnic groups continue to erupt, and in large cities and industrial centers violence floods the streets – a civil war, a war between brothers. Lovelessness is so great

2

today that on the one side people have their nice homes and secure livelihoods, while on the other side parents lay their children on the counter at the welfare center for all to see. Some live so well while millions are on the way to perpetual poverty. Let us remember what Jesus said about the end of the age: Because of the increase of wickedness, the love of most people will grow cold, and then the end will come.

Advent is a time when we await God's intervention in the need of the present day, as he intervened then in Jesus' birth. We long for the highest power to rescue this unhappy, torn humanity that knows so little community. Now is the time to ask God for a radical change in all things, even if this means we must go through judgment.

Eberhard Arnold

2

The Shaking Reality
of Advent

He has performed mighty deeds with his arm; he has scattered those who are proud in their inmost thoughts.

There is perhaps nothing we modern people need more than to be genuinely shaken up. Where life is firm we need to sense its firmness; and where it is unstable and uncertain and has no basis, we need to know this, too, and endure it.

We may ask why God sends whirlwinds over the earth, why the chaos where all appears hopeless and dark, and why there seems to be no end to human suffering. Perhaps it is because we have been living on earth in an utterly false and counterfeit security. And now God strikes the earth till it resounds, now he shakes and shatters: not to pound us with fear, but to teach us one thing—the spirit's innermost longing.

Many of the things that are happening today would never have happened if we had been living in that longing, that disquiet of heart which comes when we are faced with God, and when we look clearly at things as they really are. If we had done this, God would have withheld his hand from many of the things that now shake and crush our lives. We would have come to terms with and judged the limits of our own competence.

But we have lived in a false confidence, in a delusional security; in our spiritual insanity we really believe we can bring the stars down from heaven and kindle flames of eternity in the world. We believe that with our own forces we can avert the dangers and banish night, switch off and halt the internal quaking of the universe. We believe we can harness everything and fit it into an ultimate scheme that will last.

Here is the message of Advent: faced with him who is the Last, the world will begin to shake. Only when we do not cling to false securities will our eyes be able to see this Last One and get to the bottom of things. Only then will we have the strength to overcome the terrors into which God has let the world sink. God uses these terrors to awaken us from sleep, as Paul says, and to show us that it is time to repent, time to change things. It is time to say, "All right, it was night; but let that be over now and let us get ready for the day." We must do this with a decision that comes out of the very horrors we experience. Because of this our decision will be unshakable even in uncertainty.

If we want Advent to transform us – our homes and hearts, and even nations – then the great question for us is whether we will come out of the convulsions of our time with this determination: Yes, arise! It is time to awaken from sleep. A waking up must begin somewhere. It is time to put things back where God intended them. It is time for each of us to go to work – certain that the Lord will come – to set our life in God's order wherever we can. Where God's word is heard, he will not cheat us of the truth; where our life rebels he will reprimand it.

We need people who are moved by the horrific calamities and emerge from them with the knowledge that those who look to the Lord will be preserved by him, even if they are hounded from the earth.

The Advent message comes out of our encounter with God, with the gospel. It is thus the message that shakes – so that in the end the entire world shall be shaken. The fact that the Son of man shall come again is more than a historic prophecy; it is also a decree that God's coming and the shaking up of humanity are somehow connected. If we are inwardly inert, incapable of being genuinely moved, if we become obstinate and hard and superficial and cheap, then God himself will intervene in world events. He will teach us what it means to be placed in turmoil and to be inwardly stirred. Then the great question to us is whether we are still capable of being truly shocked – or whether we will continue to see thousands of things that we know should not be and must not be and yet remain hardened to them. In how many ways have we become indifferent and used to things that ought not to be?

Being shocked, however, out of our pathetic complacency is only part of Advent. There is much more that belongs to it. Advent is blessed with God's promises, which constitute the hidden happiness of this time. These promises kindle the light in our hearts. Being shattered, being awakened – these are necessary for Advent. In the bitterness of awakening, in the helplessness of "coming to," in the wretchedness of realizing our limitations, the golden threads that pass between heaven and earth reach us. These threads give the world a taste of the abundance it can have.

We must not shy away from Advent thoughts of this kind. We must let our inner eye see and our hearts range far. Then we will encounter both the seriousness of Advent and its blessings in a different way. We will, if we would but listen, hear the message calling out to us to cheer us, to console us, and to uplift us.

Alfred Delp

3

When the Time Was Fulfilled

While Joseph and Mary were in Bethlehem, the time was fulfilled for the baby to be born, and she gave birth to her firstborn, a son.

Luke 2:6–7

"When the time was fulfilled…" These words have such redeeming power! In the midst of our daily life we often preoccupy ourselves with those things we think serve God and his cause. We work until we are weary to the bone and yet see so little fruit. Does everything remain as it was? Haven't we made any progress? Have we actually helped at all, or have we merely scratched the surface of things? Is there any trace or glimpse of the goal we long for? What do all our efforts amount to in the face of all the forces of misery and evil in the world?

Left before such agonizing questions, it is good to remember the light that shines from the stable of Bethlehem, for it is here we are able to sense what it means that the kingdom of God came as a little child.

Christmas did not come after a great hoard of people had completed something good, or because of the successful result of any human effort. No, it came as a miracle, as the child that comes when his time is fulfilled, as a gift of the Father which he lays into those arms that are stretched out in longing. This is how the first Christmas came; in this way it always comes anew, both to us as individuals and to the whole world.

Perhaps you have waited for years to be freed from some need or sin. For a long, long time you have looked out from the darkness in search of the light. Maybe you have a difficult problem that hasn't been solved, in spite of great efforts. But then, when the time is fulfilled and God's hour arrives, a solution, light, and deliverance will come quite unexpectedly. Perhaps quite differently than you might think? Hasn't this happened to you before, just as a baby comes at his own time, and no impatience or hurrying can compel it – but then it comes with its blessing and full of the wonder of God? Hasn't God's help come to you sometimes in this way?

This is how it will be with our yearning for redemption. When we are discouraged by the apparently slow progress of all our honest efforts, by the failure of this or that person, and by the ever new reappearance of enemy powers and their apparent victories, then we should know: the time shall be fulfilled. Because of the noise and activity of the struggle and the work, we often do not hear the hidden gentle sound and movement of the life that is coming into being. But here and there, at hours that are blessed, God lets us feel how he is everywhere at work and how his cause is growing and moving forward. The time is being fulfilled and the light shall shine, perhaps just when it seems that the darkness is impenetrable.

Is it true that God only laughs at our efforts and that all our strivings cannot avail – that we are to receive everything only as a gift? How wonderful is the answer given to us by the mystery of the child! Just as the mother knows that her own surrender, care, and faithful readiness must be present along with God's working and creating, and just as every life comes into being through a working together of God and humanity, so it is also in the highest things, in the breaking in of divine life.

Yes, it is a gift when our need is relieved and the darkness is illuminated, and it is true that what is best must be given to us and that we could never produce it ourselves. But our efforts always belong to God's work, even when it is only to keep the manger prepared in which the Child wants to lie. Our deeds count, even when like Simeon we only stretch out our arms in patience and faith and in loyal endurance so that we may receive the holy gift. Even when we only wait, poor and yearning in the darkness, in fervent longing–we are ready and may help to bring about the fullness of time.

The miracle of God comes not only from above. It also comes through us; it is also dwelling in us. It has been given to every person, and it lies within each one of us as something divine, and it waits. Calling to us, it waits for the hour when we shall open wide our hearts, having found our God and our home. When this is so, we will not hoard this miracle but will let it flow out into the world. Wherever love proceeds from us and becomes truth, the time is fulfilled and Christmas comes.

Eberhard Arnold

4

God's Time

When the time had fully come, God sent his Son, born of a woman, born under law, to redeem those under law, that we might receive the full rights of sons.

Galatians 4:4–5

We can celebrate Christmas in a religious way and yet remain aloof. But when we are gripped by the meaning of Christmas all outward show disappears.

For now, however, we throw all kinds of things into the void we feel; we sense that something is missing and try to compensate for it by all kinds of expressions of love. And this is all right; in a sense it must be like this. But still in our hearts, whether we admit it or not, each of us has a deep longing to be really gripped by the Christmas message: "Christ is born! We have a Savior!"

Yet too many of us simply don't realize what we have. Jesus has become remote, and thus we are at a loss to know how to bring the birth of Christ into our lives. We certainly know how to talk about it, but how many of us possess a true feeling for it? Who of us are gripped to the point that we can stretch out our hands and exclaim: "We have a Savior!"

Oh, if God would give us something in this direction, we would be truly happy! For Christmas is a promise. The night when Jesus comes the world's darkness will disappear. When God's time comes great changes take place. Not only are the shepherds of this world startled, but the whole world – then we are shown something new.

Paul writes: "When the time had fully come, God sent his Son, born of woman."

We must not take this to mean some specific hour, like midday. God's time comes under the influence of the Spirit. Under God's direction something matures – and then the time comes. If Israel had been more faithful, the time would have been fulfilled much earlier; it could even have been in Isaiah's time. But God does not send his Son if there is no one who prepared for him. Where would he go?

For this reason God's time depends partly on us. If we follow God's word faithfully, if we understand the ways of God and hold firmly to the goal, the last days will come. Thus we should not think that Christ's birth was connected with the Roman Empire. The Roman Empire did not have the slightest significance for the kingdom of God. But whether a Simeon was there or not, or a Mary, or other people who expected God's kingdom – that was significant. Then the time could come, as it actually did. When the Word of God becomes true through faith, something is made ready in the hearts of people.

This is our hope too. Our faith is that the Savior will come soon. I am often asked, "How do you know that?" I answer bluntly, "Because I want the Savior to come soon. That is why he is near – there is no other reason!" The cause of Christ must be fulfilled wherever there are people who are waiting for it. There it will be, there it will come! That is why the time was close at hand for the apostles. And today, something toward the Day of Christ can happen if we surrender ourselves for this. Preparations for this can begin already. When it matures in our hearts, it will spread rapidly throughout the world; then the Last Day will come, the last, great Christmas!

Christoph Blumhardt

5

Prophecy

Even angels long to look into these things.

1 Peter 1:12

The mighty deeds of the future, as spoken by the prophets, fill the message of Christmas. The heavenly messengers proclaim God's rulership in their triumphant song: "Glory to God in the highest, and on earth peace to those on whom his favor rests."

Like the angels that first Christmas, the prophets proclaimed again and again the rule of God. Despite the distress of our time, we have lost touch with this prophetic spirit. In fact, the inmost nature of prophecy has become an enigma to us. We do not know its primary source anymore, and therefore we no longer grasp the demands it makes, the task it has, its impact on practical life. As far as we are concerned, the prophetic vision for the earth is a utopian dream. Only a passing fancy might still long for it feebly.

But at any moment the resplendent abundance of prophetic reality can break in upon our poverty and shame. In the prophetic word God's loving will takes shape on earth. Therefore, the prophets spoke simultaneously about the rule of God and the rule of Christ. In Jesus, the God of the stars and their heavenly hosts will begin his kingly rule on this earth, as it is in heaven.

This God has laid his Spirit in a special way upon the One who is to proclaim justice to the peoples and who will never weary until he has founded righteousness upon the earth (Isa. 42:1–4). The Spirit of God in its unique fullness – the spirit of understanding and power – shall be upon the Child, so that he can judge the needy and the poor with equity and smite the oppressors with his word (Isa. 11:1–4). His name shall be called, "God is our righteousness," because this king, like God himself, shall practice justice and righteousness throughout the land (Jer. 23:5–6). "He will judge between the nations and will settle disputes for many peoples. They will beat their swords into plowshares and their spears into pruning hooks. Nation will not take up sword against nation, nor will they train for war anymore" (Isa. 2:4). This king, who will be

as powerful and victorious as he will be just and
merciful, utterly destroys war chariots, war horses,
and war machines. "His rule will extend from sea
to sea and…to the ends of the earth" (Zech. 9:10).
"For the earth will be full of the knowledge of the
Lord as the waters cover the sea" (Isa. 11:9).

Hence Mary, in her glimpse of prophetic
certainty, exulted, "He has performed mighty deeds
with his arm; he has scattered those who are proud
in their inmost thoughts" (Lk. 1:51). It is also this
future that Simeon held in his arms: "For my eyes
have seen your salvation, which you have prepared
in the sight of all people" (Lk. 2:30–31).

The Son of Mary, God's salvation, is the only One
in whom the divine Spirit of freedom, justice, and love
finds its shape, unbroken and unhindered. Hence,
the call to repentance never ends in pessimism, but
rather in the certainty that the knowledge of God
and the liberation from injustice must go deep
and be far reaching. Jeremiah announced, "I will
cleanse them from all the sin they have committed
against me" (Jer. 33:8). And Isaiah joins in with the
jubilant cry, "The ruthless will vanish" (Isa. 29:20).
"No longer will violence be heard in your land,
nor ruin or destruction within your borders" (Isa.
60:18). "No longer will the fool be called noble nor
the scoundrel be highly respected" (Isa. 32:5). It is

so simple when in a few short words the prophet Hosea brings to expression the primal demand for this renewal of life: "Maintain love and justice, and wait for your God always" (Hos. 12:6).

This attitude is possible only when a different heart beats within us, different from that which has been in us so far, and when God's spirit dwells in us, as Ezekiel promises for these last days (Ezek. 11: 19). If the earth is to be filled with the glory of God, then the triune Spirit must fill and pervade the people who dwell on it. Only when this Spirit gains influence over us, a sovereignty thus far completely unknown, can we expect the social and moral transformation that Mary sings about.

Eberhard Arnold

6

The Wise Men's Star

When they saw the star, they were overjoyed.

Matthew 2:10

Christ looks kindly upon the wise men in the East. But let us note: in the Promised Land there is terror. Among the Gentiles there is joy; but in the Promised Land among the "righteous" there is fear! Everyone is terrified, the whole of Jerusalem is afraid. Instead of saying: "What did you say? But that is wonderful! Our promised King is coming! How great a time that will be!" Instead of this, they are shocked.

Today it is very much the same. So many good Christians are dumbfounded or tremble in fear when something of Christ's future is told to them. Granted, if this were the trembling of the heart that leads to a deeper change, that would be fine!

If we would only look forward to the Last Day with a trembling joy, as the Savior said: "When these things begin to take place, stand up and lift up your heads, because your redemption is drawing near!" (Lk. 21:28). But now, when people hear of it, they are afraid and shake and tremble. They fail to rejoice in the reality that redemption is drawing near. Salvation, salvation, salvation shall come through the promised Savior. It is not sorrow but a Savior who directs the yearning of creation. He comes to create a new world: a new heaven and a new earth. All pain and misery shall yield, and the tears shall be wiped from all eyes. Yes, we can be eager for the Day of salvation, for Jesus Christ declares only salvation.

There were people in the East who looked for salvation and whom the angel of the Lord approached. Suddenly they beheld a star before them. What kind of star? One in the sky, where everybody could see it? I don't think so. The Jews in Palestine would have seen it and inquired about it. But they didn't. This star was something to be seen and heard only by people of hope. This star was nothing else than the angel of the Lord, who must have spoken and said, "The king of the Jews is born. Go and inquire after him!" (One can see that the star was significant and must have revealed something, otherwise the wise men would not have undertaken such a long journey.) Thus, when they came to Jerusalem, they said that they had seen the star of the newborn king of the Jews.

How else could they talk like this? A small child would say: "They have talked with an angel, in the form of a star, who was sent to them by the Lord." Something has been shown and told to them, and because of this they have made the long journey and ask so confidently, "Where is he? Where is your king?" Yes—but what kind of king? Here they are held up. Nobody knows anything about it. What a shock this must have been to the wise men!

Today the Lord also makes himself known to people of hope: those who with great eagerness approach the Scriptures honestly, simply, and with purity of heart. However, those who do not look out for it do not notice anything. You can't see anything when you are asleep. Not everyone sees the star. It is necessary to have an upright, sincere heart. Whoever is not filled with longing but is only inspired by egoism, only interested in his own salvation, with no feeling for sighing creation—he will not see a star even when it is there; he does not see the glory of the Lord.

When we sigh over the misery that fills the earth, having compassion for those led astray, and our soul cries out: "Lord, show yourself! Have you abandoned your promise? Are we to hope no longer?" – then, when we stand like this before our God, a star can appear. Yes, a star of hope can be received in the heart.

The star has to appear again, but it will only come when our hearts seek it, when there is a passion for it – a sighing, striving, and aching for the great mercy to come. Yes, the star will return, and then it will shine not just for a few, but it will quickly spread its brilliance over the whole world. Yes, it is of Jesus Christ, who once appeared and will come again. The beginning was small, but great – boundlessly great – is the salvation and deliverance brought by the Savior. Yes, he comes! He comes into the world for the salvation of all – he, who is and was and will come. He comes for the redemption of sighing creation, to complete and fulfill all that was promised.

Christoph Blumhardt

7

The Crier in the Wilderness

In those days John the Baptist came, preaching in the wilderness of Judea and saying, "Repent, for the kingdom of God is near."

Woe to an age when the voices of those who cry in the wilderness have fallen silent, out-shouted by the noise of the day or outlawed or swallowed up in the intoxication of progress, or smothered and growing fainter for fear and cowardice. The devastation of our time will soon be so terrifying and universal that the word "wilderness" will readily slip off our tongues. This is already happening.

But there are still no crying voices to raise their plaint and accusation. Not for an hour can life dispense with these John-the-Baptist characters,

24

these original individuals, struck by the lightning of mission and vocation. Their hearts go before them, and that is why their eyes are so clear sighted, their judgment so incorruptible. They do not cry for the sake of crying or for the sake of having a voice. Neither to they speak out because they are killjoys and do not want the rest of us to enjoy life's pleasures. True, they themselves live on the margins of social companionship, but their comfort lies precisely in the inmost and furthermost boundaries of existence.

They cry for blessing and salvation. They summon us to our last chance, because they can already feel the ground quaking and the rafters creaking; they can already see the firmest of mountains tottering and the very stars in heaven hanging in peril. They summon us to the opportunity of warding off, by the greater power of a converted heart, the shifting desert that will pounce upon us and bury us.

O Lord, today we know once more, and in very real terms, what it means to clear away the rubble and make paths smooth again. We will have to know it and do it for years to come. Let the crying voices ring out, pointing out the wilderness and overcoming the devastation from within. May the figure of John the Baptist, the relentless envoy and prophet in God's name, be no stranger in the ruins

of our wilderness. For how shall we hear unless someone cries out above the tumult, the destruction, and
delusion?

Alfred Delp

8

The Angel of Annunciation

God sent the angel Gabriel to Nazareth to a virgin pledged to be married.

Luke 1:26–27

I see Advent with greater intensity and anticipation than ever before. Walking up and down in my cell, three paces this way and three paces that way, with my hands in irons and ahead of me an uncertain fate, I have a new and different understanding of God's promise of redemption and release.

Two years ago I was given a little angel for Advent. It bore the inscription, "Rejoice, for the Lord is near." A bomb destroyed the angel and killed the man who gave it to me. I feel he is doing me the service of an angel now.

The horror of war would be unendurable unless we kept being encouraged by the promises that have been spoken. There always are angels of annunciation,

27

speaking their message of good news into the midst of anguish, scattering their seed of blessing that will spring up one day in the midst of the night. They call us to hope. These are not yet the loud angels of rejoicing and fulfillment that come out into the open, like the angels of the first Christmas. Quiet, inconspicuous, they come into rooms and hearts as they did then. Quietly they bring God's questions and proclaim to us the wonders of God, for whom nothing is impossible.

For all its seriousness, Advent is a time of inner security, because we have received a message from on high. Oh, if it ever happens that we forget the message and the promises; if all we know is the four walls and the prison windows of our gray days; if we can no longer hear the gentle step of the announcing angels; if our souls are no longer both shaken and exalted by their whispered word – then it will be all over with us. We are living wasted time and are dead long before they do us any harm.

If we want to be alive, then we must first believe in the golden seed of God that the angels have scattered and are still offering to open hearts. Then we must walk through the gray days of our time as announcing messengers. So many need their courage strengthened, so many are in despair and in need of comfort, there is so much harshness that needs a gentle hand and an illuminating word, so much loneliness crying out for a word of release, so much loss and pain in search of inner meaning! God's messengers know that the Lord is casting seed of blessing into these hours of history as well.

Understanding this world in the light of Advent means to endure in faith, waiting for the fertility of the silent earth, the abundance of the coming harvest – not because we put our trust in the earth but because we have heard God's message and have met one of God's angels ourselves.

Advent is the time of promise; it is not yet the time of fulfillment. To eyes that do not see, it seems as though the final dice are being cast down here in the valley of death: on the battlefields, in the cities of violence and poverty, in the souls of millions who live lives of desperation. Those who are awake, however, sense the working of other powers – eternal realities, which shine their light of the radiant fulfillment to come.

From afar sound the first notes, not yet discernible as a song or melody. The new song of God's future is still far off and only just announced and foretold. But fulfillment is happening. It is occurring today. And tomorrow the angels will tell what has happened with loud, rejoicing voices, and we will know it and be glad.

Alfred Delp

9

The Blessed Woman

Do not be afraid, Mary, you have found favor with God.

Mary is the most comforting of all the Advent figures. Advent's holiest consolation is that the angel's annunciation met with a ready heart in Mary. The Word became flesh, and in the holy place of a motherly heart the earth gave birth to a world of God-humanity. What good does it do us to sense and feel our misery unless a bridge is thrown over to the other shore? What help is it to be terrified at our lostness and confusion unless a light flashes up that is a match for darkness and always is its master? What good does it do us to shiver in the coldness and hardness in which the world freezes as it goes deeper astray in itself and kills itself, unless we also come to know of the grace that is mightier than the peril of oblivion?

30

Poets and myth-makers and other tellers of
stories and fairy tales have often spoken of mothers.
Sometimes they meant the earth; other times,
nature. By this word they tried to disclose the
mysterious creative fount of all things, to conjure
up the welling mystery of life. In all this there was
hunger and anticipation and longing and Advent-
waiting for this blessed woman.

That God became a mother's son; that there
could be a woman walking the earth whose
womb was consecrated to be the holy temple and
tabernacle of God – that is actually earth's perfection
and the fulfillment of its expectations.

So many kinds of Advent consolation stream
from the mysterious figure of the blessed, expectant
Mary. The grey horizons must grow light. It is only
the immediate scene that shouts so loudly and
insistently. Beyond the present tumult there exists
a different realm, one that is now in our midst.
The woman has conceived the Child, sheltered him
beneath her heart, and given birth to the Son. The
world has come under a different law. Christmas is
not only a historic event that happened once, on
which our salvation rests. Christmas is the promise
of a new order of things, of life, of our existence.

We must remember that the blessed woman of
Nazareth, like John the Baptist and the angel of

annunciation, is an illuminating figure of life, of our existence. Deep down in her being, our days and our destinies bear the blessing and mystery of God. The blessed woman waits, and we must wait too until her hour has come. We must be patient and wait with readiness for the moment when it pleases the Lord to appear anew in our night too.

Alfred Delp

10

Christ the Lord

For unto us a child is born, to us a son is given, and the government will be on his shoulders. And he will be called Wonderful Counselor, Mighty God, Everlasting Father, Prince of Peace.

Isaiah 9:6

At the apex of our year stands Jesus, who is wonderful, a counselor, a mighty one. It is right for us now to call him our God; for in his coming in human flesh, he represents the living God of history. He is Christ the Lord. It was not meant that only one generation should boast: to us, who are born only to die, the Son of Man is born who is to live forever. As the prophets already saw it: in him the *whole world*–all generations–shall see the glory of God.

There is, however, a great distance between the birth of Christ–that is to say, between the divine life on earth revealed in him—and the birth of generations of human beings and their life today. If we survey the situation of the world, it seems that while the cry "Christ is born!" is remarkably well known, basically we are as far removed as ever from the mighty life in God. We sink helplessly into the dust when faced with the appearance of Christ. We don't have the strength to rise up to what he is and what is proclaimed of him each year.

What are we to think? Was Isaiah mistaken? Were the apostles misguided? Have we become the victims of a visionary ideal, which, though it has admittedly benefited humanity's spiritual life, has accomplished nothing fundamental in regard to a new creation?

"This calls for patient endurance and faithfulness on the part of the saints" (Rev. 13:10). For although two thousand years have gone by without our having experienced all that was revealed in Christ, nevertheless Christ was born, and he is Lord. The way that leads to him can be traveled; the obstacles along this road can be overcome; the separation between him and us can be bridged.

This is the promise of Advent. Yes, the time will come when a new humanity, born of him to true life, shall praise God on this earth. This calls for the endurance and faith of today's saints. They must defy impossibilities, looking in quiet obedience toward the words, "Unto us a Son is born." Yes, to you and to me and to all generations this Son is born. He is here. He is the Lord.

Christoph Blumhardt

11

Pure Love Alone

For God so loved the world that he gave his one and only Son, that whoever believes in him shall not perish but have eternal life.

John 3:16

In the course of the centuries people everywhere have possessed a joyful, holy expectation of a time when justice and love will prevail. Often it is only a hidden longing for unity with others. Yet through every century runs the thread of this secret hope for a time when peace and justice will come, when the Eternal One will rule completely. There is no culture on earth that has not carried this hope deep in its heart.

And now this One has come in the insignificance of lowliness, in poverty, an outcast from human society, in the feeding trough of a cowshed. He was executed among criminals by a state most outstanding in its moral and judicial standards, condemned by the demagogic voice of the people. He was killed because people did not want him to live. And again thousands of years have passed, and here and there humankind has felt and received something of the mysterious radiance of his birth.

Today people everywhere are confused, in disarray—enslaved in indescribable spiritual and emotional suffering. Expectation is far removed from fulfillment. Or maybe we haven't yet found that expectation which, in the midst of the trouble and torment, gives us a ray of hope for the future? A future that does not come from us human beings, a future that shall break in among us.

Let us try to grasp the message of peace and of Christmas, the glad tidings of God's kingdom. If we look at Jesus, the inconspicuous and lowly one, we begin to understand what expectation and fulfillment truly entail. We begin to grasp that a poor birth in a manger and a humiliating death on a criminal's cross is the only way expectation can lead to fulfillment.

Are we, too, ready to go the same way? Are we ready to go the way of love? Has this love been born in us and will we live it until death? Do we live for love, pure love alone?

Look back in history: many have gone the way of love. They discovered that the highest joy, the joy of love, leads to the goal. This joy leads to complete poverty, but also to fellowship in all areas of life. More than ever, we need people, young and old, to join together in a practical life of dedicated community founded in complete surrender. This is the way of love, of fellowship, of liberation from all need and suffering. It comes wherever people dare to drop their own fragmented, self-driven lives, their own pretensions, their own works, so as to share together a life of common work and endeavor.

Many will argue that as long as human beings are human, imperfections will result. Granted. But we should never let our longing for what is highest be held back by our imperfections. Herein lies the hope of Advent—a time when we look toward the day when all people shall become brothers and sisters because they are all children, sons and daughters of God. For in this one child, so helpless in the crib, a childlike spirit has been revealed on the earth. And this is the answer to life's deepest and most difficult questions. He alone fulfills our innermost longing.

Eberhard Arnold

Expectation

12

That Which Is to Come

…all who heard it were amazed at what the shepherds said to them.

Luke 2:18

The power of expectation is something that should accompany us throughout the year. It is with us when children are born; when the anticipation of serious trouble shakes the world; or when we are inwardly moved in a special way by our love for the coming Christ.

The so-called high festivals of the church did not originate by chance. They direct our attention to the truly important events of God's history. They point to what is most essential—ultimately to that which is to come. What is disconcerting, however, is that while the festivals and holidays go on being celebrated, their content has become so trite, so dull and superficial. Most people today would rather not think of them and cannot do so without a certain feeling of boredom. Listening to great truths and great events, and not allowing them to penetrate our hearts or overwhelm us with their force, deadens. It causes our consciences to become calloused.

This is tragic. For that which is to come – *He* who is to come – cannot really be explained in words. For those who wait, that which is to come is something that pulses through one's subconscious and unconscious being; it is an atmosphere and wave of light that reaches down to us. The feeling that goes forth from the power of what is to come cannot be described.

God's kingdom is thus a prophetic mystery. The mystery of that which is to come makes one's heart tremble in powerful joy and worship, in innermost awe and resolute readiness. That which awaits the world when it comes, when He comes, is something of immense importance. Christ's true greatness is that he is coming. Without this final future the whole of Christian faith would really be nothing.

If only our hearts were completely gripped by this! Surely, in light of what is wrong in today's world, we should all stretch out our hands toward that which is to come, so that at last the world may be redeemed from all its horrors and the dawn of

42

the new day may break. We are placed on this earth in order to proclaim, in the midst of the heaviest darkness, this message: The Morning Star has risen in my heart, in our hearts, and soon will rise over the whole of the darkened world. Repent! Believe in the gospel! He who is coming is near!

Eberhard Arnold

13

The Power of Expectation

Now we are children of God, and what we will be has not yet been made known. But we know that when he appears, we shall be like him, for we shall see him as he is. Everyone who has this hope in him purifies himself, just as he is pure.

1 John 3:2–3

Whoever lives in God does not look behind him, but forward. Whoever is alive (whoever does not fall prey to deathly atrophy of his inner life) does not look backward—be it over the short span of his own life or the greater span of history—to find a realization of his longing. He looks forward, toward the goal, toward the destiny of humanity as it should be and as it shall be. He who puts his hand to the plow looks forward. He lives "now" in the future. He who looks back and loses himself in historical speculation and his own inner reveries is not fit for God's kingdom.

The expectation of God's future is as all embracing as it is unshakably certain; it cannot be a passive waiting, a cozy and soft occupation with self and with one's small circle of like-minded friends. No, this expectation is divine power—a uniting with the powers of the future that are present here and now. This is our hope: the assurance that the social justice of the future is effective now wherever Jesus himself holds sway.

The Lord is the Spirit, and the Spirit frees us from oppression of all kinds. The spirit of expectation is the spirit of action because it is the spirit of faith. Faith is bravery. Faith is reality. He who has faith cannot believe that anything is impossible, since faith is what gives us the clear vision of life's ultimate powers. It discloses God's heart to us as the pulse of the entire living creation, and it gives us the conviction that the secret of life is love.

Anyone who lives in this love can never exhaust himself in psychological introspection or in narrow conventionality. He is concerned about the events of present history; he shares in all movements that in any way express the longing for the kingdom of the future. A person who is gripped by the experiences of faith and of love, by the expectation of

Christ and his second coming, must act. For God's love is so boundless that it applies to public life just as much as to the individual heart, to the economic as much as to political affairs.

He who has this expectation will be purified in his conscience with the purity of the One whom he expects. There is nothing that heightens the conscience more than this expectation. It eliminates all relativity. It overcomes every timid weakness, especially that indolence that causes us to throw up our arms and accept things as they are. This expectation enables us to live so securely in the future world that we, as its heralds, must dare here and now to live in accord with the unconditional character of God's future.

Advent hope is a certainty of faith that shows itself in action through mutual responsibility for the whole of life. The church of Christ is the fellowship of this hope. It believes so unreservedly that it is convinced that the divine must conquer the demonic, that love must conquer hate, that the all-embracing must conquer the isolated. Certainty tolerates no limitation. God embraces everything. When we trust in him for the future, we trust for the present. When we have faith in him, our faith holds true for everything that touches our lives.

Eberhard Arnold

14

In Holy Waiting

Now there was a man... called Simeon, who was righteous and devout. He was waiting for the consolation of Israel.

Luke 2:25

I n the Gospel we read about a lame man who waited for years by a pool, hoping to come into touch with healing forces. During all those years he was not liberated. And then healing came into his life from a completely different direction. God's power came to this waiting man through Jesus. Jesus came near to him and touched him – the Healer touched him – and in the same hour he was healed!

Thus we, too, must wait. And again Jesus will touch us, perhaps from quite a different direction than we expect; but he will come. He may or may not come in the movement of the waters stirred by the wind, but he will come and he will touch us; his strength will purify and free us.

Our world is shaking, about to erupt. Demonic powers are storming the church, like autumn storms sweeping through the woods. We live in a time when people everywhere are agitated; the masses are confused as to what is true and what is false; and yet they are waiting for what is ultimately to come. And it shall come!

The more the false prophets of today are proven wrong, the more expectation will mount. It is a good thing, then, if through hardship and suffering everything is cleared away that is opposed to God's authority. Christ is seeking a people where he alone rules–in the church and in the world.

Therefore, let us lift up our heads and look up! Deliverance is approaching. We live in the midst of tyranny, encircled on all sides, seemingly unfree. But let us lift our heads high; the hour of our liberation is drawing near. Now we must be strong in the hope that God will reveal his redemption; he who is coming will take away everything that is part of our fallen nature.

There is a story about a man who owns a garden. He comes out of his house, levels the garden, puts the paths in order and makes everything as beautiful as possible, for he expects Him, the One who is to come. He prepares everything for his arrival, because it is he who shall come!

When we turn toward the coming of the kingdom, we are living in the assurance that the powers of the future will break in at this moment. We shall taste these powers, for we are living for what is drawing near. Let us open our hearts wide, wide, for the coming One!

Now the new day of creation shall dawn for us, which is Christ's morning star!

> In holy waiting we're at home,
> The windows open to the sun,
> Though shades are spreading o'er us.
> With joy expectant hearts are fed;
> Till now hope's flaming light has led
> And brightly burned before us.

Eberhard Arnold

15

Remaining Together

*Let us not give up meeting together...but let us encourage
one another — and all the more as you see the Day approaching.*

Hebrews 10:25

The very first Christians lived in the light
of Christ's second coming. They remained
together because their common waiting
gathered them. Even before the powers of the Holy
Spirit had come upon them this gathering power
held them together like a strong centripetal force.
Their expectation was the only thing that had
gathered them. It was the strength that kept them
together, the glue that bound them, the clasp that
united them. He must come now!

The first Christians remained together and were
fully united, not only for ten or twenty days, but
for fifty days, until their expectation was fulfilled.

And such expectation will continue to be fulfilled, because it was not supposed to remain with only a few people. Here and there groups of people are to gather and pray and long for the coming kingdom.

It is not a matter of our knowing when and how God's future will come. We need not calculate or plan anything. That is nothing but foolish self-will. What matters is that we are united in the glowing center of our souls, in the very deepest, incandescent nucleus of our hearts, within the furnace of gathering expectation, within a common fire where the cold, hard iron is melted to glowing steel.

It is extremely important that in the face of the untold horror of humankind's suffering, we become one in glowing expectation, united as to which kingdom is to come and with what justice, with what peace, and with what joy this reign of God will come. Then we are genuinely gathered. Then we are melted together, fused and welded together, forged together, and loved together by the sacred spirit of this expectation.

When that happens our life will become more and more like the life that shall one day be given to all people. Our life will be a witness, a pointer to the fact that even here and now something of the justice and peace of God, the fellowship of God's people is represented. In all things God will begin to rule! We will want nothing but God's will to be done.

Eberhard Arnold

16

When the Light Shines

*In him was life, and that life was the light of humankind.
The light shines in the darkness, but the darkness has not
overcome it.*

John 1:4–5

We find it so difficult to serve God in our daily life, but this is because we don't really want to know what is true. We live in a mass of wrongs and untruths, and they surround us as a dark, dark night. Not even in the most flagrant things do we manage to break through. We are hardly repelled anymore by murder, adultery, or theft. We now have laws under whose protection one person can kill another. We have lifestyles of pleasure that poison everything beyond human repair. We have customs of acquisitiveness by which some people live at the expense of others. What can be done to help?

Throughout almost every sphere of life there is an enslaving force. It characterizes even the highest human undertakings of nations or of individuals; it is egoism. What can we get out of this or that? What will meet our momentary interest? Anything that meets our immediate needs is called good and true. Because of this night descends.

Anyone whose attention is fixed on the coming reign of God and who wants to see things change will become more and more aware that there is something universally wrong with our existence, something that is pulled over us like a choking, suffocating blanket. He will know what to do: take hold of God's hand. That will help disperse this night—at least a few areas will be made receptive to God's truth and justice and made ready to receive God himself. But to do this work we have to have a light. With this light we can then illuminate every corner where we have some work to do. Then we will see where the garbage is, where there is work to be done.

This is very hard work. But look out! When someone holds a light in his hand and shines it here and there, he is immediately asked, "What business do you have here?" That is why so many people let their light go out again. It is too awkward, too inconvenient to keep holding up a light and showing people the dirt and saying, "There, clean that up. The way you are doing things now isn't right in God's eyes. Cut off your hand! Tear out your eye! Cut off your foot!" – as Jesus says, figuratively, when there is something about the hand or eye or foot that stands in God's way.

"The light shines in the darkness, but the darkness has not overcome it." Light has a purpose: light ought to shine into our lives so that we can see what needs to be done and set our hand to it and clean it up. Jesus, the light of the world, was not well received, and neither were his apostles. "If only that light weren't there," people said. In the times of the early church, the Christians were accused of causing confusion in the world, of undermining law and religion, and were bitterly persecuted for this. The truth – the fact that our lives are not right – is too much for most of us to grasp. It seems like a crime to us to think that things we consider quite all right ought to be changed. The death of Christ, which makes it possible for a new humanity to arise in the resurrection – this sacrifice appears as foolishness.

So we turn to Sunday religion and holiday worship. God is supposed to be satisfied with that. But we know that Sunday religion is not enough. A new spirit is awakening, and there are many who seek for God's will, even though they may not know how to go about doing it. Others may polish themselves up spiritually to get their little souls in order for God. They can do this, but it is not enough. Anyone who has eyes will see this and think about how to forget himself in devotion to God's kingdom and become ardent for the reign to come.

Christoph Blumhardt

17

Get Ready for Action

Prepare the way for the Lord, make straight paths for him.

Matthew 3:3

There are many today who sigh to heaven, "Savior, come now!" But we are not sighing for the sake of God's kingdom. We cry out like this only when we are in trouble and want God to help us. We seem to know of no other help that is more effective than to have a Savior come and put a quick end to our troubles.

When it comes to the things of God, however, we must not be concerned for what is ours, but only for what belongs to Christ. We must become workers for God. This leads us to God's vineyard, a place where there is not a great deal of talk, but where we are intent on deeds.

This is what it means to prepare for Advent. Jesus says, "Be dressed ready for service, and keep your lamps burning, like servants waiting for their master to return from a wedding banquet, so that when he comes and knocks they can immediately open the door for him. It will be good for those servants whose master finds them watching when he comes" (Lk. 12:35–37). Here Jesus is speaking of his disciples and their preparation for his coming. Take note that God's kingdom is not formed by any human discovery or intention, however daring and noble, but by the coming of Christ. Our faith, our ardor, must be for this coming. Otherwise it would be better to put aside our meditations on Advent and Christmas.

It is remarkable that both God, creator of heaven and earth, and God's people must be a part of this plan. There need to be men and women who give themselves totally for God's kingdom and its justice. Otherwise Jesus would not have said, "It will be good for those servants whose master finds them watching when he comes." It is obvious that much depends on our activity. We can even read between the lines that if there is no one watching, God's coming will be delayed. If the doorkeeper does not open the door, it is possible that even the master himself, who has given him the key, cannot get in unless he forces his way.

What does this mean? We have to be dressed ready for action and have our lamps lit. In other words, while our master is absent we must be busy preparing everything in the house for his arrival and keeping everyone in the house aware that the state they are living in is only temporary.

We must also stand by the door and listen for him and open it quickly when he knocks. We must be workers dressed for service, not slackers. Slackers wear their Sunday best. A person who is getting ready to work with his hands takes his coat off and rolls up his sleeves so that he can get at the matter without further ado. God has work that has to be done in work clothes, not in our Sunday best. A practical way exists and we must be ready for this with our whole being.

Christoph Blumhardt

18

Keeping Watch

Here I am! I stand at the door and knock.

Revelation 3:20

Jesus came to this earth and then departed. But his resurrection means that God's kingdom is alive; in every moment there is something happening. He himself may not yet have come again; but he may any day soon send a messenger to knock.

For those who are listening for Christ's coming, a knock is heard over and over again. The messenger's commands are not necessarily highly spiritual. Sometimes they are very simple. We may be told, "Don't neglect your bodies. Don't you know that your body is a temple of the Holy Spirit?" (1 Cor. 3:16). "Why do you drink so much wine? Why do you eat so much food?" This seems contemptibly small. Doesn't Paul say, "The kingdom of God is not a matter of eating and drinking" (Rom. 14:17)? That is true. Yet for those who want to hear, there is a knock on the door from the coming future of Christ telling us to live for God in everything (1 Cor. 10:31). It is not only our souls that matter, but our bodies too. Whoever is wise will open the door when God's messengers speak about this. Whoever is wise will go at it joyfully and confidently.

Sometimes the knock has to do with our life together, or with the arrangements of our life in relationship to the world. For example, on a large estate there are managers, farmers, gardeners, cooks, and so on. The cook has learned cooking, the farmer farming, the gardener gardening, all according to the customary methods. They have learned their trades well and are able to carry them on, even to excel in them. But suppose there is a knock, the door is opened, and they are told, "Listen now, don't simply keep house as the world does; stop and think how to do things so as to please me!" Maybe you will answer, "What do you mean? That's the way I learned it, and that's how everybody else does it." True, everybody does it that way, but you do not need to. Those intent on Christ's coming have to bring a different way into their situations. Must things always be done in the style of the world (2 Cor. 10:3–4)? According to human wisdom? Should the kingdom of God run according to what most of us are used to?

A person who keeps watch for God, who lives for his coming, will be glad to hear even about little things like this, even if he is told, "Do everything differently from the way you have been doing it till now." When such a person hears the hint to do it differently, he will stop and listen. He will ask, "Differently? How shall I do it differently?" First you will have to become poor and see where you have acted foolishly, like someone who has no light. Then you must grieve that you are not any cleverer than anyone else when it comes to opening the door to the Master.

This is what it means to keep watch. We have to begin with what we can see. Then there will come times when we are allowed to watch for higher things. If you look for the truth in small matters you will not go astray in big ones. You will be able to recognize truth and carry out whatever commands come. Let us be staunch in our eagerness to do whatever comes to us of the truth. Then there will be knocks on our door, over and over again, and God's coming will not be hidden.

Christoph Blumhardt

19

A Savior Is Born

And being found in appearance as a man, he humbled himself and became obedient to death – even death on a cross! Therefore God exalted him to the highest place…, that at the name of Jesus every knee should bow, in heaven and on earth and under the earth, and every tongue confess that Jesus Christ is Lord.

Philippians 2:8–11

The importance of observing Christmas is not that we celebrate the Savior. The main thing is that we make our contribution among the thousands of threads woven by God, so that there are always new threads in the weaving. Christ is born. We cannot change that. We did not help bring this event about. But there were certain people – Abraham, Moses, David, and many others – who in the course of the centuries did help to precipitate this event.

The angels who appeared to the shepherds long ago may actually have been the people who in their lifetime contributed and worked towards the fulfillment of God's promise. These people live, and they are with us even now to the extent that we help bring about God's kingdom on earth. It was thus at Christ's birth, and those who took part in it rejoiced greatly. That is why the Savior said: "Abraham rejoiced at the thought of seeing my day; he saw it and was glad" (Jn. 8:56). All those who had expected Christ's coming were allowed, in some way or another, to experience his birth.

Whoever expects Christ will experience the Savior, whether he lives or dies. There is thus no such thing as death where God's kingdom is concerned. It is not a matter of wanting to leave the world behind; the one who wants to forsake the world abandons God's will. It is for this reason that God binds Abraham to his people, so to say, and his people to Abraham – they are bound together forever, down here on the earth. It is extremely important that the work of preparing the way is already undertaken on earth; it is not heaven that needs to be conquered but the earth. Would that we were all ready to focus on this divine goal!

We must ask ourselves therefore the question: "What more has to happen? What must be done

today? What can we do to bring about change?"
We should not be content with a formalized
religion; we must take practical steps toward certain
goals—toward a radical change of our present
society. Humankind has to change now, for Christ
is born.

It's all very nice to sing our songs of praise and
feel holy, but this it not the issue. No, it is a matter
of picking up the threads so that the fabric of God's
history can further develop. Our task is to find out
what we should do for God. We must begin now to
weave nets to gather people in—but understand me
rightly, not in order to convert them, they will not
be converted—but to surround them as though in
fetters and irons. There must be a people that will
capture all the rats and mice, tigers and vultures
among people, to tell them: "We have you now!
There's nothing more you can do! Jesus, whom you
have mocked is Master now!"

Sadly, there are millions of "Christians" who have
not the slightest conception of God's kingdom. We
are still holding too much to our beloved Christian
ways! We get too much pleasure out of being nice
Christians! But the crux of the matter is—are we
true prophets, or not? Are we clear about what is
necessary for the future? If we are not, then our
Christianity is meaningless. God's cause will have

to wait, just as they had to wait in Israel because the people had abandoned God's ways.

So now, this is the question: are we ready to work towards the goal which lies before us and face the judgment of a society trapped in sin? Indeed! There will be a crisis: either humankind is coming to an end, or it will be transformed and used by God! This crisis will bring the final judgment. Once we grasp this we shall be able to see the threads we are to help weave. If our weaving does not lead to this crisis within ourselves then it is not the right thread. Without this judgment nothing will change – and change it must, as surely as God is in heaven. We must keep this in plain view, so that we are no longer satisfied to jog along the old path.

While we can rejoice when people are converted, we mustn't forget that the real issue is whether there has been a confrontation, a judgment of the flesh. If we do not weave according to the threads of God's activity, we are working in vain, for *all* knees must bow before the Savior and every tongue must confess that he is the Lord. But when we tread the way of God, which leads to crisis, the whole of heaven lies open to us.

Christoph Blumhardt

20

Open the Door!

If anyone hears my voice and opens the door, I will come in and eat with him, and he with me.

Revelation 3:20

How easily we are crushed by the painful events in our lives! We bury ourselves and our thoughts in our pain instead of standing up and crying out: "What does this matter to me! To us a Son is born. Christ lives!" We prefer to find fault with our circumstances and worry about all the things that are unpleasant for us. We try to make improvements here and there; we rack our brains and wonder how we can better arrange things. All the while we are preoccupied with our future: What will happen? Will there be war or peace? Will business increase or not? Will food and housing prices rise or fall? Is the government on *our* side or not?

But is this how we want to spend our time? If we are convinced that the Son has been born to us, why do we ask these questions? Isn't he in control? When there is talk of war, believe in the Son; he also has something to say. If the nations prepare for battle, he too will be prepared. Or is it just an illusion that a Son is given to us? War or not, it is of little concern to us. A Son is born to us, and he will carry out God's will, come war or peace.

Oh, how I wish that this were uppermost in our hearts in the questions and troubles of our time, whether great or small! Instead, when trouble breaks out (which is only natural if we do not open our door to God), when some calamity breaks loose, when some evil is unleashed and threatens thousands with ruin, we allow ourselves to be captured and swept away by it. God is pushed into the background. God – who is, who was, and who shall be – is not in the first place for us. If he were, we would open the door to him in believing confidence.

But we do not really believe in him. We put more hope in the sword than in God. We expect more substantial things from human efforts than from God. We think we can obtain more from our cleverness than from God. We rely on the flesh, not on the Spirit.

There are many who struggle, but not in Christ. Storming and believing are two different things. When we storm, we leave Jesus behind, but when we believe, he goes before us. We storm ahead and say, "God be with us!" But the right thing is to believe and say, "Come! Forget everything else! We want to be on God's side. Everything we are and have must be for God."

Therefore, let each of us open the door for the Son. When you rise in the morning, perhaps already weighed down with cares and worries; when you go to bed, tired and oppressed by the day's burdens; or when you rejoice and are full of hope—in all you do, remember to stay with the Son, who lifts and bears and illuminates everything when you open the door to him. God's throne should be higher than anything else in our hearts, above everything we experience; it should rule and speak in everything that happens to us. Let us be people eager for what God wants to do. How can we be afraid, if this is how we stand?

Christoph Blumhardt

Glad Tidings

21

Where Love Breaks In

*There is nothing in all creation that is able to separate us
from the love of God that is in Christ Jesus our Lord.*

Romans 8:39

An insulating layer formed by human
thoughts and by mass impulses surrounds
our planet earth. God's spirit, God's love,
must find an opening in this layer. Somewhere, real
love, genuine camaraderie and community, and
complete clarity must break through. Somewhere
the readiness to fight against the surrounding forces
of evil must break in.

Jesus says that where two or three gather in his
name, according to his nature and in his power, he
is in their midst. Whenever God's name is called
upon, this layer is broken and the spirit of peace
and of unity bursts forth. This means that a fissure
is made in the obstructing layer.

It makes no difference where this opening is. One could say it is neither in one place nor in another. Just as cloud formations are constantly changing, so too this open place through which God's love and peace break in is not bound to any one place. This can happen anywhere at any time. It makes no difference *where* a dam is broken. Wherever it may be, floodwaters will break through. It is the same way with this flood of God's light that is trying to break in to the earth. It does not matter where this place is, as long as there is a place somewhere where love and unity break in completely and take effect.

Then something happens for the whole world! Then the kingdom of God comes close! "If I drive out demons by the Spirit of God, then the kingdom of God has come upon you" (Mt. 12:28). This is what happens when God's power breaks in. Demons are cast out. The power of evil spirits is broken and driven away. The Holy Spirit creates a pure atmosphere, one of unity and of peace.

The little stable in Bethlehem was a place where God's love broke in. While on earth, Jesus expected God's kingdom to break in. His expectation was that light must break in upon this darkened earth. He saw that death had heaped up a barrier so that light could not come into life on earth. Therefore he sacrificed his life so that in the area of death an opening might be made; so that there might be a rift in the layer of fog around the earth through which the light of God could come in. If a house has even only one window where the sun shines in, it can no longer be dark inside the house.

If Jesus opens a breach in death then God's kingdom comes down to this earth. This was the faith that the early Christian church had when they waited for the Holy Spirit at Pentecost. They were determined to wait until the flame of the Spirit, like the star over Bethlehem, should come down at this one place. And this did happen; it came.

From the place where a stream enters, it pours out into the entire world. Where love breaks in, all other forces yield. Jesus was victorious on the cross, not by a greater force, but by a greater power – the power of love – in comparison with which all force is nothing. No human force is able to achieve anything in comparison to the power of love.

Eberhard Arnold

22

Before the Manger

He came to that which was his own, but his own did not receive him.

John 1:11

Why is it that the holy, silent night of two thousand years ago, this night which millions have been singing about and believing in for two thousand years—why is it that we go through this night just as we go through every other night of the year? Why does the stable of Bethlehem with its wonders and history stand there, while so many of us pass it by as if it were an ordinary stable like any of the thousands of stables on earth?

If we truly look at the mystery of this night in a personal way, pray over it, and reflect on the real meaning of our lives, then we will know that the mystery of this night leads us to an encounter with the Absolute. As such, we will be shaken up. For when we stand before the Absolute, what is genuine and real is revealed. If we fail to be moved when we come to the manger, something ultimate is missing.

Let us be genuine before the manger. For faced with the Absolute, only final things have worth. All our words, the façade, playing on emotions – all these fall away. Only what stands upright and is final and authentic counts here.

How many of us, in our good-hearted way, have ridden past the stable on the high horse of our opinions and convictions, leaving the Child behind, not realizing he was there? How many of us have stood up for what we believed, even in defiance, but were not awake to the fact that we were riding past a miracle – the miracle of life and love?

Before the Absolute we should become witnesses, giving testimony to what is true. But this can only happen if we are touched in our inmost being, trembling before him in our deepest heart. At the manger we fall silent, worshipping and wondering.

How are we to come to the manger and discover its message? How are we to perceive what is asked of us? How are we to find the Child? Consider who was at the manger – the shepherds and the wise men of distant lands. There were no businessmen, no politicians, no scholars. Those with great power

were missing; the great adventurers of the spirit
and of earth were not there. Where were they? The
manger was empty of them.

But the shepherds were – those of unschooled
plainness and simplicity, healthy and unspoiled.
They were plain folk, untwisted and unspoiled by
the sophisticated, who still had their instinct and
taste, not yet ruined by a hundred degeneracies and
a thousand opinions. They were still able to perceive,
to taste what happened. They had judgment of their
own and did not have to refer to a thousand books
or turn to hundreds of authorities. They themselves
could smell things, so to speak.

Because of this they sensed that here was the
miracle, here was the Lord, here was the place to
bow down. Let proud Jerusalem stand there; let
thousands of high priests be; let the mighty keep
aloof; let Herod's sword rattle. The healthy person,
the one with taste and style that come from blood
and heart, will simply sense that here is the mystery.

And then there were wise men – those who by
long seeking and searching and waiting and enduring
became inwardly honest and ready. These were not
shrewd, crafty intellectuals. No, they were men
who saw the greater relationships and not merely
the things that are isolated and lost in themselves.
They were ones who could sense from a thousand

indications where the ultimate decisions lay, why they must be made, and where the genuine questions were to be asked, and where an answer could be found. Here were human beings willing to risk and venture to break camp and to go wandering through deserts, to leave for far lands and go seeking because they were determined to find what was ultimate.

An entire nation, a whole people can walk past the manger. So, too, an entire epoch can pass by this manger. But there the shepherds and wise men stood in wonder and prayer – they would not fit into a conventional standard. They were straight-forward, wholesome, and seeking. Not only did God become human so that we might become God, as the old saying goes. This other comes first: God became human so that we might be able just to remain who we are created to be: human.

Before the manger many things are decided. Much more than we might think. It is not an idyllic scene; it is humankind's hour of destiny. Not for nothing is it said, "The kindness and love of God our Savior appeared" (Tit. 3:4). For us individually it is truly important that we sense that in this manger lies a love, a salvation, for us, for all humans, for the world.

Alfred Delp

23

Let Our Hearts Be Moved

But Mary treasured up all these things and pondered them in her heart.

Luke 2:19

The call to repentance always has to strike our hearts anew. All our spiritual resources and capacities must be set in motion in quite a different way than they have been up to now. No human being has so few gifts that spiritual powers cannot be given to him. But our hearts must be set in motion. Only a spirit that is moved is capable of work. An unmoved spirit is like unmoved heat over the desert. The desert remains unfruitful. It makes no difference how many or how few gifts we have; if the Holy Spirit does not empower our gifts, we are unfruitful.

What we need in this time is the work of the Spirit. Here is the amazing tension. Fundamental truth is unchanging; but we can only come into contact with it to the degree that our hearts are stimulated, moved, and changed by the Spirit. Truth is alive only in love.

Unless our hearts are moved, they are cold. When our hearts are cold, we think and talk about our own personal weaknesses and those of others, because our hearts are not gripped by the greatest love of all. Then we are inclined to dwell upon whatever we find irritating in others. But when our hearts are alive to God's great plan, by which He rules over all space and all worlds, then we are living in the love that moves God's heart.

God's is the only heart that is really great and deep. God's heart is forever moved because God is love. And when we live in this love we are freed from all petty thoughts.

The call to repentance by the prophets is precisely this call: let your hearts be moved, for mighty things are before you! And when Jesus took up this prophetic call, he proclaimed that the kingdom of God was at hand! A message of joy is coming! The deeds of God's kingdom are happening! Get ready!

Jesus said, "If I drive out demons by the finger of God, then the kingdom of God has come to you" (Lk. 11:20). "Now it is really in your midst, for I am!" This is what Jesus' first followers experienced. Through his presence the reality of God's kingdom was present. Wherever Jesus was, all other spirits were overcome.

In this way we can grasp Jesus as the mighty one who takes up his dwelling in our hearts. I am in the midst of your house! With his coming, God's kingdom with all its powers is working among us. We are able to live in accordance with it and tread all other spirits underfoot, yes – even tread Satan underfoot! This is the task of the church.

The church is therefore a fighting church. It lives completely in God's future, in the great facts and events that become manifest in Christ's final coming. It has received God's kingdom into its midst already now through the pouring out of the Holy Spirit. For the Holy Spirit is the pledge for our redemption. He is the seal on the promise of God's kingdom, the vanguard of the kingdom of the future, the presence of Jesus.

So let us enter these days of Christmas and with all our hearts ask God to move us with his thoughts: that we may think along big lines, not only in continents, not only in planets, but in the largest constellations; that we may think not only in cycles of years, but in decades, centuries, and millennia, in the dimensions of God's thoughts, in God's great sweeping curves.

Let this be our concern this Christmas time. It is a serious one, a challenge to us. Let us not be a small generation met by great things. Let us become worthy of a great time and a great calling.

Eberhard Arnold

24

Born unto *Us!*

Today in the town of David a Savior has been born to you; he is Christ the Lord.

Luke 2:11

There is no event in the history of salvation that so expressly calls forth joy as does the experience of Christmas. Into the world of fear and worry, right into the midst of all our troubles, comes the proclamation of great joy, "Today a Savior has been born to you!"

The coming of the deliverer among people who groan under their need in loneliness and death must truly be a source of abundant joy. One is born who brings us the greatest thing of all: fellowship with the living God! Here is One who through his life and death brings God to all those who are willing to accept him.

Christ's birth was a prelude to his death. The lowliness of his birth, the immediate persecution by Herod, and the terrible massacre at Bethlehem—these are the signs over the manger signifying the life that awaited him; they are the sign of the cross. But they are also the sign that the broken bond between us and God will be restored.

This brings us great joy! Here is someone who will sacrifice everything in order to free us and redeem us. This little child is our Savior because he is born to redeem us from our sins. His life and death, the action of his spirit, proves that he is the Son of the living God. This is the gospel: what was promised through the prophets is the Son who in the flesh is born of the seed of David and whose power is proven as Son in the spirit.

This living, risen Son can only be known by faith. "The real, blessed faith that God's word and work demands," Luther says, "is the firm faith that Christ is born for you and that his birth is yours, that it took place for your sake; for the gospel teaches that Christ was born for our sake and that he died and suffered all things for our sake. The angel does not merely say that Christ is born; he says, For *you,* for you he is born. He does not say, I bring news of great joy; he says, To *you,* I bring you news of great joy."

The birth of Jesus took place under the sign of light. If we want to become united with the One who was born, we will give ourselves wholly to him – with all our sins! For, as Luther reminds us in the old words of the mystic Angelus Silesius, "Were Christ born a thousand times in Bethlehem and not in you, you would still be eternally lost."

For Luther the Redeemer is identified with the sinner. "See, Christ takes our birth from us to himself and immerses it in his birth and gives us his, so that in it we might become pure and new, as if it were our own. Thus every Christian may rejoice and glory in this birth, as if he, like Christ, were born of Mary." Therefore, Christ must become ours and we his. To us a child is born, to us a son is given. Born to us, to us, to us!

Eberhard Arnold

25

A New Message

The shepherds returned, glorifying and praising God for all the things they had heard and seen.

Luke 2:20

What was it that made Mary, Joseph, Zechariah, Elizabeth, Anna, Simeon, and so many others wait for the kingdom of God and receive something from heaven? Surely it was nothing but the great heart God had given them. It was through the Word of God that they were given marvelous thoughts and were made mindful of the great promises. They were consumed with grief for the misery of their whole people and the whole world, but they were also made firm in faith by the words of God's promise.

If we want to be a people of God, we too must come to see and hear something of God. And if we are a people of the covenant, then we are also a vessel for God's speech and for the outpouring of the Holy Spirit, since the Bible says that God himself will teach every person. We should thus long to hear God's voice again, long to experience the life of the risen Christ, long for the power and light of the Holy Spirit to be made visible again. It is a sign of how blinded we Christians are, that not only have we not experienced anything for centuries, but we do not even believe there is a need to experience anything new.

But we will not let our joy be taken from us, for we know that there is great rejoicing in heaven. We know that Jesus is being praised throughout all the heavens, especially in our times, when we have signs that great things are happening. And so we rejoice with all the heavenly hosts and will not be led astray—even if most people never think of the great things of God but just go on in the same old way with their Christianity, as drowsily one year as the next.

People's hearts are stirred—by what? Test it and see. By nothing but earthly things! Their minds are stirred—by what? By profits! There are political interests, social strivings, all sorts of alliances among people, church controversies in which people are full of fire about all sorts of forms and doctrines, and feel themselves very important. Yet we are just poor worms that do not even realize what a mess we are in.

We desperately need a new message, a new speech, for so few of us have the joy of Christmas. Let us do everything we can to prepare for a time when new lips will be given us. The joy of God's people must be brought to light. The Lord will yet reveal himself, and there will be signs again that show us where Jesus is to be sought.

Therefore, let us take Christmas into our hearts and be glad! Let us be happy, though there is still so much darkness on earth! We will be joyful in hope, glorifying God, and we will not waver! Let us stretch out our hands to the things that are above, where Christ is sitting at the right hand of God. If we are faithful in this we will be made ever more free in the spirit.

Christoph Blumhardt

26

Peace on Earth

Glory to God in the highest, and on earth peace to all on whom his favor rests.

Luke 2:14

God's will finds its simplest expression in the words: "Peace on earth." God wants peace. The kingdom of God is constantly working towards this one goal: peace on earth!

God's peace, however, is different from what we understand. In times of war we groan: "Oh, if only there were peace again!" Yet we are only wishing things to be as they were before. The peace of God goes much deeper. God wants to do away with all the strife and misery. Human contention is but a sign that our hearts are not at peace. Moreover, the entire creation also yearns for peace. The prophets, whenever they speak of peace, include the whole created order – the animals shall also find peace, and the plants, and all living things shall be brought together so that there may truly be peace on earth.

For this reason, our longing for peace should extend far beyond the time when guns are silent and we cease to kill each other. There is much, much more at stake. Human peace, in which the nations give up war "for a while," is never enough. The peace of Christ is greater than all our understanding and cultural achievements; for even where we work hard for harmony, strife among us and in our families breaks out far too easily. What we need is deep-rooted reconciliation in Jesus Christ – God's peace for us all, changing this earth into heaven.

Pain, sadness, death and destruction are every-where. The last enemy who must be overcome is death. Not necessarily our death, meaning our departure from this earth, but death as the darkness in our hearts, that dreadful and terrible evil which separates us from God and each other and prevents us from receiving the light we need to work for eternal things. All this must come to an end.

"Death, I will be poison to you! Hell, I will be a plague to you!" Thus speak the prophets, because God's will is peace. So long as death and damnation hold us in thrall, and so long as everyone is seeking their own self-interests, we will not have peace.

We have to be among those who fight for God's light. When the angels proclaim: "Peace on earth," then hallelujahs should rise up out of our hearts, and we must say: "Yes, Lord God, and we want it too! We don't want death or sin or hell to destroy us! We are with you, Lord God, our Father. We are one in heart."

We must be strong in our hearts and hold on to God. "I will make a covenant of peace with humankind and all evil shall cease to be, and all sin and death shall come to an end" (Ezek. 34:25). We will not live in fear and trembling, but stand steadfast and true until all that is broken on earth is healed.

Christoph Blumhardt

27

Truly Christ's Day

For my eyes have seen your salvation, which you have prepared in the sight of all people.

A very small-minded way of thinking has overtaken us, where everybody thinks pretty much of himself: Unto *me* is born a Savior! Look. How the Father in heaven has opened up the treasury for me!

Such petty thinking is all wrong. Jesus' birth is not something that happened for the good of your soul or my soul; it is something that happened for the good of God, the good of creation, the good of every living creature. It is something that happened to bring God's glory to light in a great, vast world that stretches through heaven and on earth and under the earth.

This is what should move our hearts at Christmas time. Christmas is a time when we can forget ourselves and think about our Savior. Let us not be lazy Christians, doing nothing but celebrate. Let us work, let us suffer and endure, and even die for our Lord Jesus. Let our only concern be to see that his work goes on; that the glory of God is spread over all people; that the streams of the Holy Spirit come again and we walk in newness of life.

This is something we can not just preach. It is something we should consider quietly by ourselves. True, Christmas has now become a holiday for everyone, that is, a Christmas-tree holiday. Crowds of people are excited about this day, but without knowing exactly why. Hence they squander their earthly life on temporal things, doing the best they can. There is nothing much we can do about this; we just have to let people go ahead. Nevertheless, we should be seized with compassion for the millions of people who, with the best of intentions and to the best of their understanding, use up their strength on matters that don't count. This alone should compel us to seek for something higher from God.

There is much we can do in quietness to serve God, if we gather around the manger like the shepherds of Bethlehem. Let us not falter just because there are only a few people who praise God in this way. It can only be a few; there never will be many. God's flock is a little one and always will be. But this flock has to give itself for the whole world, for the living God, for everyone's sake, just as a few despised shepherds had to be there on behalf of all people to see and hear the choirs of the heavenly host and pass on to us the message of peace.

The joy of the shepherds was not that they were the ones who had heard the angels and seen such a great thing, but that a new light was given to the world, that God had visited his people again. We too must prepare ourselves as a people united with God through Christ. Then we will be ready to receive grace after grace, revelation after revelation, for the world and for humankind, to the glory of God. This is what our joy should be, and it is our joy on this day. Truly Christmas – Christ's day – belongs to both heaven and earth.

Christoph Blumhardt

28

The New Time

I have come into the world as a light, so that no one who believes in me should stay in darkness.

John 12:46

On Christ's birthday let every person believe that Jesus helps us. The living Jesus will come to us and make something out of us. He is God's pledge of help. For this reason the angels proclaim, "Glory to God in the highest, and on earth peace to all on whom his favor rests."

It is true that what the angels sang has not happened yet, but we can hope for the time when Jesus will appear, and then we will say: "I was dead, but lo, I live!" We can hope for such a time. It must come, it will come, and we rejoice about it, and we wish to honor the Father because of it. This must be our delight, consolation, and strength. Our greatest hopes for ourselves and for the whole world to come from Jesus, and in him we fortify our spirit against all evil.

In the end no devil and no hell and no damnation will count. Jesus alone has the right to claim all people for himself by the right of God's love and mercy. The earth itself shall rejoice, and the trees and grass shall rejoice over Christ, and he must not be robbed of a hair's breadth. No person, no sin, no death, no devil, no Satan can take a thread from him in this world. All things have become Christ's in the love of the Father.

It is tragic that so many people no longer believe that God is love; Christ has been represented to them as their damnation. Our heart's greatest cry to God must be: "O Father, let false Christianity be exterminated, so that the voice of your Son might be heard—for we have so much religion that our Savior is no longer heard." Let us pray that Christ's voice is heard again. For no hell, no sin, no death counts, because Jesus lives! This has to be proclaimed on the day of his birth, and nobody will be put to shame who exalts and honors Jesus. He is the Lord who is, who was, and who will be, to the honor to God.

Christoph Blumhardt

God with Us

29

Immanuel

...and they will call him Immanuel – which means, "God with us."

Matthew 1:23

"*Immanuel! God is with us!*" We proclaim this fact in the sense that God's love includes the entire world! One can't even cross a street today without meeting people whose ideas and outlook on life are different. You can't travel to any place without mixing and living with people who are different. If God is with us, then he must also be with them! If we think we have to wait until they are converted or changed, we'll most certainly be least in God's kingdom. Jesus died for us because he died for the entire, godless world. *This* is the love of God: he bestows a kiss without waiting until we have become angels! If God is with me, he is with all people! God is with us – all of us!

If we are honest it is not easy to identify with this Immanuel. It would be so much simpler if I could just stand in a niche near my Savior and be "saved" and let the world go to hell – that's not hard. But to accept Immanuel and proclaim, "God with us," and be entirely sure that the world belongs to God, and get to work, that's difficult. Much of the world doesn't want anything to do with God. Worse still, even the followers of Jesus hardly understand what it means that the world belongs to God. Christians not only take up arms against "unbelievers," they fight one another and kill each other and consign one another to hell – that is sheer torment.

Jesus, the light of the world, Jesus, the love of God for the world – these must be put into practice! "Immanuel!" Let it be today, tomorrow, and for all time: "God with you, with me, with all the world!" In this way we can be, "people for life"; and wherever we go, wherever we stay, we can say "Immanuel." When things are hard for us, when we meet enemies, let us remember *Immanuel* and be joyful that this Savior came into the world!

Christoph Blumhardt

30

The Struggle of the Atmospheres

This is the verdict: Light has come into the world, but people loved darkness instead of light.

John 3:19

Humanity is stretched out between heaven and hell. Not only are human beings a tightrope between the animal world and that which is spirit, we are like a vault stretching upward and outward between two atmospheres. Yet neither the one nor the other of these atmospheres is outside of this human vault; both are within us. This is an awesome situation, and we are placed in it to fight.

The one atmosphere is poisoned and brings death. It often possesses a deceptive character, appearing very much alive, even beneficial to life. It can be compared to tuberculosis; the patient tends to seek the very stimulants that destroy his vital energy. This is what characterizes decadence, corruption, and degeneracy – the fact that corrupt life craves those poisons that destroy it. And the uncanny thing about this death-bringing atmosphere is that it sparkles with all the colors of life. This sham life, which is actually dead, is the dangerous enemy that besets us. It is contagious and lethal.

What are we to do? The whole earth is shrouded in this atmosphere; all of human life is penetrated by it. There exists an earth-spirit, a spirit of this world, a spirit of the age, and it influences all we do. We usually fail to notice the potency of this atmosphere and how it destroys. We are as used to it as we are to the stale air in rooms where the windows are opened only once a year. In fact, we feel quite uncomfortable when any fresh air is let in. It's as if all the coziness is gone.

Christ's atmosphere is pure, clear, fresh, creative life. This pure air is alive; it brings vitality and energy. This clear atmosphere is true. It makes life upright and straight and thus truly alive. It pulsates with joy in all living things, and in this joy it brings new strength again and again to the lives of others. This atmosphere unites everyone who lives in it, all who breathe the common air of living fellowship.

Just like the other atmosphere, this atmosphere also fills and penetrates all things.

Unless we learn to distinguish between these two opposing atmospheres, we cannot enter into the battle that takes place between them. Nor will we have the right weapons with which to fight. For guns and bombs and barricades are of no use in this battle. Neither is our own moral strength.

In ourselves, we have no power or authority over these atmospheres. For polar tensions exist, so to speak, tremendous tensions between our guilt and our longing for God. At times the poles are so far apart that we can scarcely hope for lightning to flash between them. And yet just then it will flash—all the stronger, the further apart the poles are.

We are placed right in the middle of these two atmospheres. This is an awesome reality in our lives, so tremendous that there are times when we want to despair or to flee. And yet we cannot escape; for these atmospheres are at work everywhere, wherever we go, whatever our attitude.

This is why Christ came; this is why the Son was born and the Word became flesh: that the pure atmosphere from God might become revealed as it truly is. But more, that this atmosphere might grip us and flood through us. For though people love the darkness, in Christ's birth the atmosphere of light and life breaks in. Through it we are led to life.

The Spirit, the atmosphere that brought Christ – this same Spirit through his resurrection overpowered death. This Spirit brought about the birth of Jesus; the Word became flesh. And then, upon his death, the Spirit lifted the stone, opened the grave, and snatched Christ from the grave. This same Holy Spirit brings to us the power of resurrection.

The power of Christ born of Mary, the power of Christ hung on the cross and risen from the grave, streams out to us in the Holy Spirit. The power of him who is victorious over death and the devil now makes us ready for the struggle between the atmospheres. This is given to us through the Holy Spirit.

In a mysterious way the Holy Spirit is especially present in the unity of believers. In this unity we are taken out of the realm of darkness and placed in the atmosphere of light. "The darkness is passing and the true light is already shining" (1 Jn. 2:8). We are no longer bound to do the works of darkness; we have taken up the weapons of light, for now we are led, guided, driven, and inspired by the Holy Spirit. This alone confers the victory on us.

Where the two atmospheres are still at strife with one another, all creation groans, all nature sighs as we do for redemption by the Son of God, for the liberation in which the Son of God shall be known, for the atmosphere of the childlike spirit, of the freed spirit. All the unchildlikeness that still lies heavy upon unredeemed nature groans and sighs for this redemption of God's children, for this redemption by the Holy Spirit, for this childlike freeing in which Christ's power of resurrection will be shown.

And yet, despite the groans and sighs, nothing, as Paul exclaims, nothing can separate us from God's love. Not the infernal forces of the abyss; not the powers of this world, the social and political and economic and religious powers; not the spirit of mammon and of deceit. We are victorious through the love of him who has loved us, through this atmosphere filled with the authority of Jesus Christ. This is the victory. Light is stronger than darkness. God's love overpowers death and all the spirits of death.

Eberhard Arnold

31

The Hour of Decision

Then Herod called the Magi secretly and found out from them the exact time the star had appeared... And having been warned in a dream not to go back to Herod, they returned to their country by another route.

Matthew 2:7, 12

We live in a desperate hour, when the very opposite of unity and love has been lashed into the greatest fury by the demons. Soul-killing materialism, infidelity and impurity, deceit and ungenuineness — when we pretend to be something different from what we feel in our hearts — shape the bulk of our lives and choices. Therefore, nothing is more needed than unity in love — a unity that allows nothing to thwart or prevent us from becoming one heart and one soul.

The hour of decision has arrived for the world. Even the blind have to see this. Therefore it is important now to gather, though not for our own sake. As with the ark, our hope is that we may reach the other shore and lay the foundation for a new world. It is a matter of life or death, of love or hatred, of God or Satan; it is a matter of decision.

Our challenge is to live a life of truth, a life that is genuinely free, a life that is moved by conviction, a life in which our actions truly reflect what we believe. Of course no one is perfect. Our hearts are a battleground between good and evil. All the more, we must live by what the best voice within us says, we must strive after what is holiest and brightest and nurture the most lucid part of our heart.

The mysterious men from the Orient followed the star and discovered the place where the secret of love lay in the helplessness of a human baby, wrapped in swaddling clothes in the feeding trough of an animal. They discovered the place where God's love came down. That is the most important thing for every person, to discover in his own time and at his own hour the place where God's love has broken through, and then to follow the star that has risen for him and to remain true to the light that has fallen into his heart.

The birth of God's Son is God's challenge for each of us to manifest his love. There is no manifestation of love quite so complete as that of a life lived in unity and community, a love where houses and doors and hearts are kept open for all.

Let King Herod come then with his threats and drive from the land those who follow the star, who have come to the star of love. Let him even drive the divine Child himself out of the land. It makes no difference to those who follow the star. The angel of the Lord will protect the revelation of love in the midst of times of the greatest hatred and of the heaviest darkness and gloom.

Eberhard Arnold

32

Away with Human Honor

And they bowed down and worshiped him.

Matthew 2:11

We dishonor God most deeply when we give honor to people and receive honor from them. We should give each other love, not honor. All honor belongs to God alone in Christ.

Honoring Christ means that he is different from us, that we are not worthy to tie or untie his shoestrings or to clean his shoes or do him any other service. We must recognize how unworthy we are to be one of his followers. Nobody is worthy to work for him, to live for him, to do anything for him. Christ alone is truly empowered by God, truly endowed by God.

Christ is the ruler, the king, the exalted! He is exalted because he took upon himself the ultimate humiliation; no one can reach to such a depth from such a height as Jesus did. He showed us that he has God's interest, that he is the heart of God, because he went the whole way from the greatest height to the lowest humiliation.

Jesus shows us who God really is. He wants fully to accept us and our service, though we are not worthy of it and cannot be praised for it. Jesus teaches us that when we have done everything, we have not done more than we ought to do.

So away with all human honor! Then we will have room and space to honor him whom we love. We honor Christ in the expectation, the recognition, the knowledge that he is coming, he who is Lord over all. We honor him when we recognize that no power is so great, no dominion so secure as his. He will topple the lofty from their thrones and raise up the lowly. That will be his work when he comes.

Eberhard Arnold

33

God in the Flesh

The Word became flesh and made his dwelling among us.

John 1:14

Do we in reality experience that God came in the flesh? We should not think this matter is closed with the birth of the Savior. Nor should we imagine that because Jesus died, rose again, and ascended into heaven it is now our duty to celebrate the birth of Christ. Our risen Lord does not care much whether we celebrate his birth, whether we immortalize the Child in the manger or not. What matters to him is not our belief that he was once born but that we realize that he is here, now! He wants us to grasp that "God in the flesh" is true now.

"God is in the flesh"; this alone can raise humanity, and with it all flesh—the earth, the whole of creation—to a height that we have not yet attained.

Granted, there are powers of opposition at work. Our human condition, full of sin, full of misery, full of death, full of unclarity, makes it difficult for us to believe that God is here among us. Our flesh is filled with darkness. We know all too well how succumbing to our flesh leads to murder, theft, and all kinds of blasphemy. Nevertheless, "God became flesh!"

"God in the flesh" is our weapon against all that is fleshly, whether we call it death, the devil, or darkness, or sin. Whatever we may call it, it is that part of us we long to get rid of. There is good in all of us, but as much as we want to be good we can't. I want to serve truth but am driven by deceit. I want to be just, but in so much of what I do I am unjust. I have the will, but I am unable to carry it through. Many of us condemn ourselves because of this. We're all told to fight against our fleshly impulses. Well, just try to fight it! For centuries people have studied, have invented ascetic practices and self-torture to put an end to their fleshly desires. It has all been in vain. No person can humanly wage this fight.

Yet a fight has been launched by the One who came and still comes in the flesh. The God who came in the flesh is the devil's most powerful adversary – the devil who exploits our flesh. Christ opposes our injustice with God's justice. It is he who takes up the fight against sin, the fight of life against death. This battle is truly being fought, and it will lead to victory.

Through grace we need not give in, nor do we have to get discouraged by our human condition. We are not just miserable creatures or lost sinners. Our fallen flesh is deceitful in nature. When we live in sin, we fail to live as God created us. Therefore the words "God in the flesh" mean that we can become *truly* human again. It is not true that we belong ultimately to sin. What is wrong in our flesh is not final! Only when God dwells in me am I fully human!

In this struggle our fists, our intelligence, and our understanding are of little use. All our efforts accomplish little. Left to my own resources, I cannot get a hold of sin and drive it out. Nevertheless, I can say to sin, "Your end is prepared for you. It will come as surely as I live because God is in the flesh." Were he not in the flesh today, I would rather give up my faith. If I cannot have God fight in my flesh, then all is lost.

This is why Christ's day, Christmas, is so significant. Christ did not come and dwell amongst us to be our teacher or our tyrant. He came to be our redeemer. He came to overcome all that is not of God. Therefore, I no longer need to fear my own sinfulness. No. For then Christ would not be in the flesh. And since Christ came into this flesh of ours – this body in which sin and death dwell – I am free! Even though I am still a sinner, I am free. The victory is on my side, on your side. Only believe it, carry it in your hearts. Nothing else is needed.

Christoph Blumhardt

34

Jesus and the Poorest

You know the grace of our Lord Jesus Christ, that though he was rich, yet for your sakes he became poor.

2 Corinthians 8:9

Jesus—the eternal Word—was born in a cattle shed and laid in a manger. As a man he unashamedly said: I have no bed, no roof over my head, no pillow. I am homeless. And when he died, he humbled himself even more and became a "criminal." He was executed between two robbers, one on his right and the other on his left, like a criminal. Even his clothes were taken from him.

Why did Jesus—God's very heart—become so poor? This question is decisive, because he calls us to go the same way. He wants us to live even as he did. His way means to leave everything and to sell everything, to become completely poor with him. Why all this? The answer is clear. He had to make himself poor and low, otherwise he would not have been able to reach us – the very poorest and the very lowest.

Jesus sought out the poor. He did not seek the rich. He lived and taught an all-embracing poverty, which included both material and spiritual existence. Without the gift of the Holy Spirit we can do nothing of lasting importance. Thus we read at the beginning of the Sermon on the Mount in Matthew's Gospel: "Blessed are the poor in spirit," the beggarly poor in regard to the spirit. In the Gospel of Luke, Jesus speaks of material poverty: "Blessed are you who are poor," in contrast to the rich. Jesus loves the poor – those who feel their utter need for God.

Jesus thus situates himself as the very poorest among the poor. He seeks even to share their way of life. He wanders as they do. He takes food and water as they do, as with the Samaritan woman at the well. He sleeps as they do, or is sleepless as they are. He spends the night on the mountains and in the boat on the water, but all this with God. For he did all this through God's love. And so he concerned himself with the whole person, not only for the soul and the innermost feelings, but also for the body and all its needs. The poorest, the sickest, the most insane of people were close to him. And he healed them all, as far as they had faith. He even raised the dead.

Jesus always sought out the lowest, the "sinner." "I did not come for the good and healthy, I came for the sick and the sinners. I came for the poorest people" (Mt. 9:12–13). And he, who well knew what money and injustice mean, loved the tax collectors who took unjust interest. And he, who well knew what it means to sell one's body for money and give it over to impure spirits, loved those who were known throughout the city to be vile – such women were allowed to dry his feet with their hair. Everywhere he associated with the marginal, yet never doing the evil they committed.

In Christ – and particularly the Christ child – all human pride was cast down, and all degradation was raised up. Mary and Elizabeth had already recognized this in their songs of praise before the birth of Jesus. And why? Because the love of God cannot be revealed in any other way! When the Holy Spirit was poured out upon the early Christians, no one was able to keep his possessions to himself anymore. They surrendered everything – just as Jesus did at his birth.

Jesus came to this earth to bring God's love to needy souls, to the lowliest people. Only so was he able to reveal the justice of God's kingdom. For in

God's kingdom there is no other justice than that which is mercy for the poorest of the poor. In Jesus there is no other way to effect peace than by taking a stand against riches and for the poor, there is no other love in Christ than by taking upon oneself the need of the poorest and never forgetting it.

Eberhard Arnold

35

The Living Reality

No one has ever seen God, but God the One and Only,
who is at the Father's side, has made him known.

John 1:18

We humans can recognize things only by their opposites. Thus we see light by its contrast, darkness. So, too, the light of Christ's coming and of his future becomes especially evident by way of contrast with the dark state of the present world. Such contrast brings the nearness of Christ's coming: The light shines into the darkness, which does not receive it; yet neither can the darkness overcome the light.

In the book of *Revelation* John describes how he beheld the approaching Day of judgment and in contrast to it God's throne of light, the throne of his world of stars, the throne of the four living creatures and the twenty-four elders, the throne in whose midst the Son of man, the Lamb of God, is revealed as the being of light, of all eternal light. In his vision we see the forces emanating from this throne, the fiery torches and the seven spirits of the Holy Spirit, the crystal sea and the entire revelation of God's will and of God's heart. We see the throng of martyrs and the multitude of the glorified members of the church. And then, like John, we sense the sinister consequences of divine judgment that must come on the whole earth. The powerful and the great on earth must be brought low; all injustice must be taken away; all violence and all wickedness must be laid down and what is degraded must be lifted up. We witness how the Spirit of the future lifts up the humbled throng of the believers.

What was given to Mary, the faith given to her to receive the eternal Word by the action of the Holy Spirit, this action is identical with the Spirit's action in the church. Jerusalem, the city of the dwelling places above, the holy city-church at God's throne, the city which at the end of John's Revelation was shown to be the kingdom of God—this city is now at God's throne in the heavenly dwelling places.

And from this city on high, from this church above, we receive the life of Christ, the true life that is from God. It is from there that we receive forgiveness of sin and the true gathering and uniting in God's peace. From there we receive the actual possibility of making God's kingdom a reality on this earth.

How important and significant it is that Christ's reality cannot remain invisible, in some so-called invisible church. No. The powers from on high must come to visible expression. Boundless grace is given to us so that we might manifest the invisible mystery right here on earth; we can become a living representation in time and space of what is holiest in the highest.

Let us hold, therefore, to the certainty that the invisible shall become visible. And it shall be placed and built into this world; it shall rule over this temporal order, and in this way the body of Christ, the church of God, and his coming kingdom shall be seen.

Eberhard Arnold

36

Humiliation

He has brought down rulers from their thrones but has lifted up the humble. He has filled the hungry with good things but has sent the rich away empty.

Luke 1:52–53

It is those who are lowly and unworthy in the eyes of the world who are called by God to do the most vital task on earth, that is, to gather his church and proclaim his gospel.

Again and again, what it amounts to is a clash between two opposing goals: One goal is to seek the person of high position, the great person, the spiritual person, the clever person, the fine person, the person who because of his natural talents represents a high peak, as it were, in the mountain range of humanity. The other goal is to seek the lowly people, the minorities, the handicapped and mentally retarded, the prisoners: the valleys of the lowly between the heights of the great. They are the degraded, the enslaved, the exploited, the weak and poor, the poorest of the poor.

The first goal aims to exalt the individual, by virtue of his natural gifts, to a state approaching the divine. In the end he is made a god. The other goal seeks the wonder and mystery of God becoming man, God seeking the lowest place among men.

Two completely opposite directions. One is the self-glorifying upward thrust. The other is the downward movement to become human. One is the way of self-love and self-exaltation. The other is the way of God's love and love of one's neighbor.

Jesus experienced the utmost humiliation. From the feed-trough and the manger at his birth to his death on the cross. May we return again to the only thing that counts: to the way of Jesus Christ who was humiliated, tried, and crucified with criminals for our sake. We want to ask God to let us become like Jesus and, like him, to revere the childlike spirit of love and humility.

He who reveals God as a man, this is the One whom we seek. He who reveals God as love, this is the human being with whom we want to have communion. He who associates with the lowliest, he on whom the Holy Spirit of God descends, him we mean.

We pray for the whole human race to be released from the folly and delusion of exalting "wonderful" people. We pray that they may see that the meaning of history and the meaning of every human life lies in Jesus Christ, who is the new Man. Through him and in him humankind will be renewed. And this renewal will begin in the body of Christ, which is the church.

Eberhard Arnold

37

The Motherly Spirit

Mary… was found to be with child through the Holy Spirit.

From the Christmas Gospel we know how Mary, with a childlike faith, received the Word, and in this way the incarnation of the eternal Spirit came about. In the time of the early Christians, too, we hear about this faith. May we grasp this mystery with the faith of the heart. For the mind alone can never penetrate these things. It is not a matter of agreeing or disagreeing. We have to stand before God's secret with reverent awe and experience in our own lives this miracle of the incarnation.

Let Mary, the mother of Jesus, teach us to become more childlike. For Mary is the image of the heavenly life-giving mother, the church. Again and again we have to receive in our hearts this heavenly virgin – the motherly, womanly spirit of the church community, the upper Jerusalem, the power of the church as it is living now. It is not that we simply become the heavenly church, but that we receive it in its perfection. The more we receive the life-giving strength of the bride of Christ, the more we shall radiate in our lives – however weak we are – the wonderful unity that came from the birth of Jesus.

Mary was sealed with the Holy Spirit as soon as she believed. In this way the Word took on human nature from her. Through Mary's simple faith she received the Spirit and thus conceived Christ, and he was born of her. Those who want to be reborn must, like Mary, first hear the Word and then believe it. And then, in the humility of Jesus and of Mary, we must learn to occupy the most modest human place in loving, devoted, long-suffering and in the freedom of joy.

He who would be born of God must be mindful of how Christ's birth took place. All birth from God happens as it did with Christ. When the Word is heard and when it is received, then faith is sealed with the Holy Spirit. This Spirit renews every person and makes us alive in God's justice. We become a new creature, a new creation.

Eberhard Arnold

38

New Birth

Mary was greatly troubled...

Luke 1:29

In pure, opened hearts the Word wants to become flesh and life. This takes place, however, with great fright and trembling, as it did in Mary when she heard God's will from the angel. In us, too, the Word must be born. In us, too, this cannot happen except through pain, through poverty and misery, inward and outward.

New birth brings new life. When the Word is born, when it becomes flesh in us, then we live for love and its fruit; then we live only for God.

The Christ child born of the virgin Mary therefore serves as a pattern for all new birth. Christ's birth is not only our pattern or example; it is a miracle that happened once and yet still occurs ever anew, even though in an entirely different way. Every baby born to followers of Christ should be born out of the mystery of the Spirit and pass through the life of the church to the final mystery of the kingdom. This is so wonderful and glorious that we can only marvel at it.

It is not surprising then that when a newborn comes into the world, the father and mother themselves may experience a renewal of inner growth. Every baby should turn us to the mystery of the birth of Jesus whereby an entirely new beginning is made through the Holy Spirit, just as it was with Mary.

Through Mary the incarnation of the Word took place. With us weaker human beings the Word comes in a different way: The ever-renewed birth of the Christ child in our hearts remains as decisive for our lives as the ever-renewed acceptance of Jesus' teachings, of his miraculous power to heal and to drive out wicked spirits of temptation. This birth is as decisive for our lives as the ever-renewed acceptance of Christ's death on the cross and his resurrection. It is as decisive as the ever-renewed decision to follow his life. It is as decisive as the ever-renewed acceptance of the Holy Spirit, the Spirit in whom the whole future of his tremendous reality in his coming kingdom is given to us.

Eberhard Arnold

39

The Incarnation

Now you are the body of Christ, and each one of you is part of it.

1 Corinthians 12:27

Today, as it was two thousand years ago, Christ wants to enter this world. It is for this that the Holy Spirit is sent from the throne of the Father and of the Son. It was for this that on the cross Christ broke down the fences and walls – so that he may be embodied anew among people: the church (Eph. 2:14–16).

The living Word once took on flesh in Mary's son. The eternal, living Word – Christ – now takes on a new body in the church. Therefore the apostle Paul said that a mystery was entrusted to him, which he calls the body of Christ (Col. 1:24–26). The fact that the church is the body of Christ means that he becomes visible and real in the world.

Thus in his letter to the Colossians, Paul speaks of "the mystery" of the body of Christ, "which is Christ in you," and refers to the expectation of Christ's future coming – the "hope of glory" (Col. 1:27). The "hope" is the expectation, the assurance of a completely new order. And by "glory" Paul means Christ's majesty in his accession to the throne. This is the glory: that God in Christ really rules over all things. All political, social, educational, and all human problems are solved in a concrete way whenever Christ rules.

There is a reason why talk about the future coming of Christ fades away in people's ears today. What is needed is action, not theology. Something must be established, something must be created and formed so that no one can simply pass off the reality of Christ's incarnation. This is the embodiment, the corporeality of Christ – the church.

Just as Christ was in Mary, so Christ wants to live in us who believe and love. If Christ is real in us then we will live in accordance with and reflect the character of God's future. This is not something moralistic or legalistic; it is something organic. It takes place now, through Christ in the church. The future kingdom receives form in the church.

For this reason the church must represent now God's peace and justice in our world. This is why it must be free of all actions by which human individuals are made great. This is why it cannot shed blood or tolerate private property. This is why the church cannot lie or take an oath. This is why it cannot tolerate the destruction of bridal purity and of faithfulness in the marriage of two people. This is why it lives as simply as possible in order to help as many people as possible. This is why the church expends all its life and energy to make room for God to bring everything under his rule.

Eberhard Arnold

40

Christ Must Enter Again

Since the children have flesh and blood, he too shared in
their humanity.

Hebrews 2:14

I f Christ has been born to us, we have to get busy. It is up to us to prepare the way for Christ's coming. We must open wide to him the door into our current situation, even if we have to give up everything. One thought alone must possess us: Enter, you Man of the Most High, you Man of life, and take hold of us for the almighty God. Judge and winnow us miserable, lost people until the new life that you have brought us is born in us.

We are called to prove in our *own* lives that Christ is born, that God is with us. But we are constantly in danger of going about our business without Christ. We keep to our old ways of life and do not allow God to enter our daily affairs.

This should deeply pain us, for there should be far more than a handful of people who believe in him; the good news must take hold of far more people who in turn will rattle at the door to throw it open to him who is born to them. We should never rest until all obstacles are cleared out of the way for him who is born to us, and who is to come.

But too many of us are frightened of what the future may bring. The hammer of hostile forces is battering at the door of the nations. Our life is threatening to go to pieces. And in the face of all this, we feel so utterly helpless. What are we to do? Should we not be frightened, be anxious? Perhaps. But we will not despair. Even in our fear we will cry out: "Unto us a child is born!"

We will always have to struggle to make sure that Jesus enters our lives and lives *on earth,* not only in heaven. This is the fight of the church in the world. We are placed in the restlessness and the anxiety of a world fraught with evil, but we have a battle cry and the joyful news: "To us a Son is born!"

Christoph Blumhardt

Epilogue

In light of the holiday hoopla that surrounds so much of Christmas today, celebrating Christ's birth has become an outright anomaly. One of the most special, holy, and radical events in history has become the greatest marketing gimmick in the world. Most of us cannot—or will not—deal with this contradiction. Hopefully this collection has helped us to do so. Yet, despite ourselves, for reasons other than the joy of giving, too many of us spend too much money on gifts that people don't need.

Why? Why has the holiday rush all but replaced the miracle wrought by God's spirit? If we are honest, the real meaning of Christmas makes us nervous. It unnerves us because the Infinite, who came in a feeding trough, is not the kind of God we want. Such a God is too powerless for our liking; he's too much like the people we don't want to be, but actually are.

In an age of technological prowess and material prosperity, we despise being powerless. Humility we can handle, but stark naked vulnerability repulses us. Our lives and society are built on successfully maneuvering our world into a position of safety, secure from the contingencies of existence. We are taught to be always in a position of strength. We want power to accomplish, actualize, maximize, and materialize, and in so doing we expend a great deal of energy negotiating what we want and how to get it. Yes, negotiate. In countless ways we finagle the means necessary to protect and expand the turf we call *"my own."*

As much as we might hate to admit it, remembering Christ's birth interrupts our very *modus operandi.* That's why, as Dietrich Bonhoeffer put it, Christmas is "frightening news for everyone who has a conscience." Deep down, we resist receiving the One who unveils our weakness. We don't want to admit our need for God, let alone for anybody else.

The Christmas story tells us that God chose the way of descent and emptied himself of his divine prerogatives in order to indwell our nothingness, our darkness. Mary's womb, barren, lacking Joseph's potency, becomes home for the naked God. Christmas is thus the story of the God who is conceived in barren space, who is born in the unwelcome place of an empty manger.

Christmas is not just the message of light breaking into darkness (a truth-deposit that has been universally recognized throughout the ages) but a humiliating fact: foolishness to the "wise" and a stumbling block to the "righteous." The God who saves is beggarly; he exists in weakness and comes to those who reach up to him with empty hands. Such a God is an embarrassment, not just to the Herods of this world, but to all who are enamored with themselves and with their own achievements.

We don't want this God. We prefer the glorious deity of splendor who dazzles our eyes but also blinds us from seeing our lives for what they are. We don't want the bloody babe who later is condemned to die, defamed and disfigured, for the reason that we don't want to come to terms with the stable of our own existence. We have an inn to offer, decorated for Christmas, not a stinking stall. We have cathedrals to worship in, not barns.

And so, we too easily let Christmas move on by. We quickly forget about it until "next year," as if it were just a matter of history. In so doing, we fail to experience how God in Christ wants to enter time and space today. We miss the power that turns our worlds upside down and inside out, where "valleys are made high, and mountains are laid low." We rob ourselves of *God's* gift!

If Christmas is to go beyond sentiment and merriment, if it is to impact our lives beyond a certain season, then we must realize again and again, in the words of J.B. Philips, "the awe-inspiring humility of God." Christmas means coming to terms with who we are and the way our world is, and it means repenting for who we try to make God and ourselves to be. Only this realization can lift us out of all that destroys our world.

Martyred priest, Oscar Romero, wrote shortly before his death:

> No one can celebrate
> a genuine Christmas
> without being truly poor.
> The self-sufficient, the proud,
> those who, because they have
> everything, look down on others,
> those who have no need
> even for God – for them there
> will be no Christmas.
> Only the poor, the hungry,
> those who need someone
> to come on their behalf,

will have that someone.
That someone is God.
Immanuel. God-with-us.
Without poverty of spirit
there can be no abundance of God.

Christ's birth should lead us to recognize our beggarly existence. This, strangely enough, is good news. For, when we are weak, as the apostle Paul writes, we are strong. Only then will God come to us. Then having a Savior will arouse joy, not just a nod.

Jesus' birth points us ultimately to his death and thus to his resurrection. Christ's life is a seamless whole. We honor his birth, therefore, not only when we prepare for it and celebrate it, but when we take up his cross and follow him to Golgatha – the lowliest of descents. But herein lies the greatest news of all: Christ was born to conquer death; in him is new life. Christmas is the beginning of a downward journey that leads us to the end of ourselves and to the gift of new life. This is why Jesus was born in a manger, lived in poverty, and died on a cross. The humiliation of God is our hope for a new world.

Charles E. Moore